CHRISTIANS *in* Danger

CHRISTIANS *in* Danger

Twenty Reasons for Hope

Marc Fromager

Scepter

This is an updated translation of *Chretiens en danger: Vingt raisons d'espére*r published by Editions des Beatitudes, S.O.C., copyright © 2013.

P.O. Box 1391
New Rochelle, NY 10802
www.scepterpublishers.org

Cover and text design by Rose Design

ISBN: 978-1-59417-231-1

Printed in the United States of America

Contents

Introduction

The subtitle of this book, *Twenty Reasons for Hope*, might seem paradoxical or even contradictory with regard to the main title, *Christians in Danger*, which is all about peril and distress. But this apparent oxymoron is no mere attention-grabbing literary device. It is literally true: Yes, Christians are in danger in many countries around the world, and yes, there are reasons for hope.

The discrimination suffered by Christians often goes completely unmentioned. Plenty is said and written about every other kind of victim—this really is the era of victims—but, surprisingly, Christians seem to be treated differently. In spite of objective, plainly verifiable, and stubborn facts, the topic remains globally taboo.

In the time of the Soviet Union, the persecution of Christians by the Soviet dictator was passed over in total silence, including within the Church. Since the fall of the Berlin Wall, a polite veil has been drawn over this subject. People seem to feel that there is no point in reminding anyone about it, because, after all, it is past history. In short, it has not been discussed either during or after the events—in other words, never.

There are several possible explanations for this selective denial of reality. The likeliest is our rejection of our own identity—our history, our culture, our religion, and our country. In this mental construct, not only are people totally unconcerned about anything bad that happens to Christians, but, over and above that, people refuse to talk about persecution because that would involve criticizing the "Other," who is by definition a paragon of all virtues. To talk about persecution implies the existence of persecutors, whereas, in the fantasy world of reality-denial, everyone is nice, so there cannot be anything bad anywhere.

Talking about suffering—and what is more, the suffering of Christians—seems like a mere persecution complex. Yet the briefest look at what is happening in the world is enough to show that it is real, and very widespread. It is estimated that 200 million Christians, or 10 percent of Christ's disciples, are not completely free to practice their faith.

Among them there is, of course, a wide range of situations, going from covert discrimination to the most violent persecution, but all of them have to pay some kind of price for their faith. For some of them the price is very high indeed. This book, which describes a very small number of these situations, is dedicated to them.

The choice of countries aims to be representative of the various environments in which these people live, with a geographical spread over all the continents except Australasia (which is less involved) and illustrating various different sources of discrimination, whether political or religious.

◆ ◆ ◆

To return to the subtitle of this book, *Twenty Reasons for Hope*, each chapter ends with a look to the future based on hope. This opening up, as a sort of counterpoint to the suffering previously described, is not the fruit of a fanciful optimism that ignores reality, but is backed up by a degree of evidence, drawing conclusions from certain developments.

Of course, no one can prophesy, and every attempt to predict the future is necessarily limited, but I thought it was important to think about the future of these countries, short- or longer-term, and of the Christians living in them.

Twenty countries have been included, one of them being France, which may seem surprising. I felt it was necessary to include countries of long-standing Christianity; I could have taken another Western country as my focus, but I had to make a choice. It goes without saying that the situation in France is not as dramatic as in most of the other countries presented in this book, but it seemed relevant for one Western European country to figure in the book, since they are being progressively subjected to anti-Christian persecution, too.

The list is not, unfortunately, exhaustive. Very many other countries could have, even should have, been described. As a director of Aid to the Church in Need (ACN), I have had the opportunity—or rather the privilege—of meeting these communities more or less everywhere in the world, and these Christians *in danger* have much more to give to us than we can give them. They know in whom they have placed their trust, a trust that does not deceive.

I would like to assure the Christians who have been left out of this book that they are not forgotten. I know that they, too, share in the hope that is its underlying message. In that way too, they surpass us. In fact there are as many reasons for hope as there are witnesses, and the number of witnesses is past counting!

I
PART

The Middle East

1

Saudi Arabia

Apparently the name *Red Sea* was due to the reddish reflections of Mount Sinai—or was it a reference to the blood of the Egyptians at the time of the Exodus? Gazing from the window of the airplane from Beirut to Jeddah, I am trying to use distractions like these to deal with my anxiety.

A Somewhat Un-Catholic Visa

It is not the airplane that worries me. I make plenty of flights every year. It is my destination. After all, for the director of a Catholic organization for the relief of persecuted Christians to go to Saudi Arabia is necessarily a bit of a risk. But my real worry is about my passport: the visa is not in my name.

At the Saudi Arabian Embassy in Paris, I had to fill out an online form at the last minute, and I put the name of my sponsor, the person who officially invited me to the country, in place of my own name. Therefore the visa was issued in my sponsor's name, while my passport was in my own name—but it was the day before I traveled and too late to change it.

On checking in, and again on embarking in Beirut, our visas and airline tickets were checked. Although the name on the visa was not mine, after a moment's hesitation I was allowed to board. All that remains is the arrival at Jeddah, which is now worrying me greatly, making me think that maybe my wish to discover what Christians are going through in this country was not my best idea ever. In the end, mysteriously, everything is fine. Afterward, embassy staff point out the discrepancy to me on several occasions, and it is put down to an administrative error.

The Church of the Catacombs

Jeddah is a port: in other words the sort of town that is traditionally fairly open to the rest of the world. That is certainly the case here, where Jeddah's difference from Riyadh, the capital since 1986, is very marked. Jeddah is also, however, the port of entry for travelers to Mecca, which is close by. Pilgrims used to arrive by boat; now they arrive by air, in such vast numbers that one of the terminals is reserved for them alone.

Finally I get things sorted out and am able to meet the people I have come to find, first in Jeddah and then in Riyadh. In 1976 there were 200,000 Catholics on the Arabian Peninsula. Now there are three million! The number of Catholics, then, is fifteen times bigger than thirty years ago, undoubtedly the steepest increase in the world.

But in Saudi Arabia absolutely everything is forbidden. No church, no Bible, no rosary, no crucifix is permitted; nothing referring to Christianity is allowed into this country, which sees itself as one big shrine to Islam. Here, Christians are officially forbidden any possibility of the sacraments or communal prayer. Officially—because, in fact, there is a completely underground Church.

I have never before met truly clandestine Christians. I have read accounts of life in the Iron Curtain countries, but I came along too late to meet them *in situ*. Now, in Saudi Arabia, I listen to the people who organize, in a completely invisible way, the life of the little communities that make up the local Church, the Church of the catacombs. Within a century, and I hope even before that, films will be made of these heroes of the faith and the unbelievable daring of their mission.

They are mainly Asians: Indians, Sri Lankans, Pakistanis, and Filipinos—Filipinos like those in the churches of Tokyo, Istanbul, or Stockholm. Filipinos are to be found everywhere, and often they are the pillar of the parishes in countries where Christian communities are marginal, or even marginalized.

By meeting in small groups in each other's homes, these Catholics are taking real risks. If they are discovered, they can be imprisoned and physically attacked. Whatever happens, it means deportation or the nonrenewal of their work permit—and thus the end of their livelihood.

Going to Mass in these circumstances implies deep faith and a real hunger for the Eucharist. When young people in Western countries have to be coaxed and begged to go to Sunday Mass, it would sometimes be a good idea to remind them that, in some parts of the world, it is not merely a social rite or a habit, but a dangerous undertaking that requires a good deal of courage—and this courage can only be explained by the crucial importance these people give to the Eucharist.

The permanent threat is from the *mutawa,* or religious police force, which is all-powerful. Charged with ensuring absolute conformity to the rigorous Wahhabi interpretation of Islamic practice, the *mutawa* supervise everything in the public space and enforce conformity by beatings—whether closing shops at the times of prayer, or the apparel of women, all of whom, including foreigners, must wear the Islamic veil and the all-enveloping garment known as the *abaya*.

A French woman I meet there is wearing a badge that says: "Delete me." And that is exactly what happens: Women are deleted. All one sees is a crowd of cloned shadows, with black being the norm.

For men it is white, which makes the dress code nice and simple. The whole country is dressed in black and white, a fair summing up of a deeply binary nation. You are either Muslim or non-Muslim, either man or woman, either master or slave. In each case, you are not really a person unless you belong to the first category!

The Islamization of Saudi Arabia as it is today came about in three waves. After the conquest of the Peninsula by Mohammed and his armies, and then the alliance in the eighteenth century between the Saudi family and the Wahhabis, the last quarter of the twentieth century saw a growing stranglehold on the part of the religious leaders, who demanded concessions at the times of the Iranian Revolution and the Gulf War. Whether because of competition from Shiites or the massive presence of American soldiers on Saudi soil, Saudi Arabia was determined to remain *the* world reference point for Islam.

This became still more important because of the "organic connection" between Saudi Arabia and the United States ever since the 1945 agreement reached on board USS *Quincy* between King Ibn Saud and President Roosevelt, ensuring Saudi stability and the supply of oil to the United States. This alliance with a partner from outside the *ummah,* or community of Muslims, was less surprising than it may appear, since puritan Protestantism and Wahhabi Islam had many elements in common: their (official) aversion to alcohol, prudishness, militant millenarianism, and extreme legalism.

Today there seems to be some desire to moderate this stranglehold, particularly in the field of education (revision of syllabuses, opening of mixed universities, opening of two new schools every day) and the law (creation of some civil tribunals in addition to the Sharia courts). But in the traditional Bedouin way, there is a culture of consensus that needs time. Everything moves very slowly.

Christians, moreover, are not the only ones to be kept under strict surveillance. Shiite Muslims, who make up about 10 percent of the population, are considered as, at best, heretics, and at worst, non-Muslims. This question is a constant source of tension, especially since 30 percent of the people in the oil-producing eastern part of the country are Shiites.

◆ ◆ ◆

In May 2011 the Catholic Church in the Arabian Peninsula was reorganized. Until that point, Saudi Arabia, Kuwait, Bahrain, Qatar, the United Arab Emirates, the Sultanate of Oman, and Yemen were included in one Apostolic Vicariate under the responsibility of the bishop of Abu Dhabi, Msgr. Paul Hinder, a Swiss Capuchin. He could truthfully be called the bishop of six nations, covering three million square kilometers, with a Catholic population of about three million souls (i.e., one Catholic per square kilometer)!

In May 2011, however, the Vicariate was divided in two, and Msgr. Camillo Ballin, the Italian bishop of Kuwait City, took over responsibility for Kuwait itself, Saudi Arabia, Qatar, and Bahrain, where he now lives, since the Kingdom of Bahrain is the most central country of the new Vicariate of Northern Arabia. In February 2013 the King of Bahrain gave Msgr. Ballin some land for a new cathedral. Now all he needs to do is build it!

He has already created three parishes in Saudi Arabia, although they are still at a fairly theoretical level since there are no actual buildings. Each of these parishes covers an area bigger than France. The parish of Jeddah, whose territory includes Mecca and Medina, is dedicated to Our Lady of Arabia. "It's up to her to prepare our path!" explains the bishop.

Conversions to Christianity

In that sort of context, what good news can there be? Surprisingly, while the Middle East is, catastrophically, being emptied of its native-born Christians, new Christians are settling in the region, repopulating communities that were rapidly disappearing over the past few decades, or had vanished over the centuries.

It is important, nevertheless, to remember that a large part of the Arabian Peninsula was covered with Christian churches and monasteries before the arrival of Islam. In the course of archeological excavations or, more prosaically, the preparation of building sites, people uncover the foundations of ancient churches whose existence had been forgotten or deliberately obliterated.

So the situation is that on the Peninsula from which all traces of Christianity disappeared thirteen centuries ago there are now three million Catholics. History is coming full circle in an almost comical way, all the more so since the atmosphere is not exactly propitious. Even so, with the exception of Saudi Arabia itself, new churches are now being built—not nearly enough, admittedly—including one in Qatar, inaugurated in 2008, and very soon another in Bahrain.

Comparing the proportion of mosques in Switzerland to the Muslim population there (I'm taking Switzerland for my example because the bishop of Abu Dhabi is Swiss), with the proportion of churches to the Catholic population of the Peninsula, it can be seen that the supply of churches in the Arabian Peninsula is forty times lower than the supply of mosques in Switzerland. And yet a Saudi sheikh recently issued a *fatwa* calling for the destruction of all the churches on the Peninsula.

That being the case, the new Catholic inhabitants, mainly Asian (the Peninsula is, after all, part of Asia) are only there provisionally for work; they will return home when their contracts end. But the real good news is the conversion of a growing number of Muslims to Christianity in the very heart of the Arabian Peninsula.

There is one thing I should explain at this point, to avoid being accused of undermining interreligious dialogue. It goes without saying that I am in favor of dialogue, because in today's world there are only two options open: either conflict or dialogue. A third option, indifference, is no longer available, because globalization has brought us into daily contact with each other's beliefs. Neither can this be used as an excuse for the sort of relativism that would prevent one from choosing any religion at all.

As a Christian, it is absolutely clear that I believe Christianity is the true religion, revealed by him who described himself as "the Way, the Truth, and the Life." It is equally clear that I would like my own joy in knowing the Risen Christ to be shared by as many other people as possible. As a result, it seems to me that, although we should have the greatest respect for believers of other religions and for nonbelievers, as Christians we can only rejoice at the increasing number of conversions to Christianity.

Faith is a gift from God, but on the Peninsula this grace seems to come via two main channels: the media and dreams. The proliferation of Christian TV and radio channels in the local languages (Arabic, Farsi, Turkish, etc.) and the development of good-quality programs on the Internet mean that more and more people can discover Christ's message, which is obviously and powerfully attractive.

Then there are dreams, which to us, with our rationalistic Western outlook, seems really surprising. Asians seem to have preserved a certain spiritual sensitivity that makes them more *permeable* to the world of divine things. Today there are endless accounts from people who had a dream, either sleeping or waking, during which they experienced the presence of Christ or of the Virgin Mary in some way. Conversion does not happen instantly or automatically, but whatever path it takes, grace opens up the path for the journey to Christianity.

However, it is still very difficult to give any figures for conversions, because they are normally confidential for reasons of security. People are generally reluctant even to confide in those closest to them. Personally, I am convinced the day will come when crowds of people who have been converted will arise—people who have been practicing their faith in secret until that moment—and that, in spite of the martyrdom that will undoubtedly be inflicted on their forerunners, we will only be able to feel astonished gratitude for their numbers and for the quality of their faith and fidelity to Christ, which has been tested by fire, however secretly.

It will not only be in Saudi Arabia or the Arabian Peninsula. A sheikh recently expressed alarm at the fact that in Africa six million Muslims are being converted to Christianity every year. What about France? It is too soon to answer that—you'll have to wait for the last chapter.

2

EGYPT

New Year's Day 2011. I was running rapidly over the news headlines first thing in the morning. Suddenly I felt that I was in the middle of a nightmare: a church in Alexandria had been attacked.

I don't say that we at ACN had foreseen the Egyptian revolution that would break out three weeks later, but we had already seen clearly that 2011 was threatening to be a bad year for Christians in Egypt.

For that reason we had planned to increase our reporting about Egypt considerably, and for that same reason I was at the point of booking a flight to Cairo, wanting to be there, together with our brothers and sisters, on the first anniversary of the massacre of Nag Hammadi (Upper Egypt), where six Coptic Christians had been shot down as they came out of Mass on January 6, 2010. I simply had no idea that our premonitions were going to be fulfilled so quickly and so dramatically.

Three days later I was in Egypt with some ACN correspondents. All over the country, people were talking about the attack. Egyptian Christians were shocked by what had happened and exasperated by the failure of the Egyptian authorities to protect them despite the permanent threats to which they were subject. However, they were not surprised by it, since they were, unfortunately, getting more and more accustomed to the climate of violence.

On our way to Christmas Mass, which is celebrated in the East on the day of the Epiphany rather than the Nativity, we could not help feeling somewhat afraid. We got there early, not only to get a place, but also so that we were not too near the doors, just in case. . . .

"In Ten Years, There Will Be No Christians Left!"

The name *Copt* is ultimately derived from the Greek *Aigyptios*, or "Egyptian." Today the Copts are eager to maintain their historical roots, being descended from the ancient Egyptians of the times of the Pharaohs and considering themselves to be the "real Egyptians."

However, without being entirely "second-class citizens," it is abundantly clear that they feel more and more like foreigners in their own country. Moreover, everything possible is done to remind them of it, in a thousand small, everyday things. They are a minority with a major handicap in the eyes of other Egyptians: They are Christians.

It is very difficult to accurately determine the number of Christians in Egypt. They are mostly Orthodox, and the Orthodox Church, based on its parish registers, claims to represent between 15 and 20 percent of the population. The government, meanwhile, estimates that Orthodox Christians account for between 2 and 3 percent. The conflicting figures speak for themselves.

In reality, it seems as though Orthodox Christians may make up about 10 percent of the population of Egypt, or around eight million faithful. As for Catholic Copts, the picture is similar, though on a much smaller scale: estimates vary between 150,000 and 250,000 people, with the median figure of 200,000 being likely closest to reality. This would mean Catholics make up 2.5 percent of the Christians and 0.25 percent of the overall population of the country.

The Egyptian Orthodox Church refused to recognize the Council of Chalcedon, which condemned monophysitism, in 451. Some think this refusal was due to mutual misunderstandings—people saying the same things, but in different ways—and political causes: Alexandria resented being demoted from the position of second-ranking Patriarchate in favor of Constantinople when the Roman Emperor moved there in the fourth century. This is all very far removed from the Gospel, but we may see some points of resemblance between the actors in these historical events and ourselves.

Official relations between Catholic and Orthodox Copts are at best indifferent and at worst frankly deplorable. I mentioned "foreigners" just now; that is exactly how the Orthodox see Catholics. There may be friendly contacts between some of them at the personal level, including bishops, but cooperation is zero. In certain parts of Egypt, there is even friction. Some Catholic bishops have told me they have more difficulties with Orthodox Christians than Muslims!

The fact is, however, that the difficult overall situation of Christians cries out for them to be reconciled to one another. The atmosphere in Egypt, without being actually hostile, is definitely worrying.

"On paper, if things continue as at present, in ten years there will be no Christians left in the Near East, including Egypt!" declares Msgr. Antonios Aziz, bishop of Giza. But he remains confident. He reckons that statistics have their place, but they don't determine the future. Bishop Antonios cites the example of the diaspora of Egyptian Christians who have emigrated. Statistically, the sizes of the diaspora communities should have diminished as second and third generations became assimilated into their new countries. But instead they continue to be deeply attached to Egypt, and they are very active in supporting the Church in Egypt financially and even politically, by lobbying the governments of the countries where they are present in the greatest numbers—the United States, Australia, and countries in Europe.

The fact remains that difficulties and violence are a permanent feature of life. To build or even renovate a church, planning permission has to be obtained, which is perfectly normal. But it almost never arrives, which is abnormal. Planning permission is also required for mosques, but they are usually built before permission arrives (Egyptian bureaucracy seems rather slow), secure in the knowledge that no one is going to demolish a mosque! For a church to be built, the permission of the provincial governor also has to be obtained, and this slows things down even more.

A further problem is that when a request is submitted for permission to build a church, it often happens that a mosque is very quickly built as close as possible to the proposed site, making it impossible to build a church there. Existing churches always have one or more mosques close by—to such an extent that someone offered me a remarkable new definition of the word *church*: "a building surrounded by at least four mosques"!

At school, history textbooks simply jump over the first six centuries AD. They go straight from the Pharaohs to the Islamic conquest, the "liberation" from Roman occupation. Christian identity and Christian history are buried in silence.

In public employment, the figures are eloquent. Christians make up 10 percent of the population and just 1.5 percent of civil servants. Even allowing that a minority should be represented by a minority, the deliberate sidelining of Christians is clear evidence of discrimination. In reality, the mere fact of being a Christian means one has seven times fewer chances of getting a job of any kind. And if one does, there is no point hoping for a promotion or the chance to exercise any kind of responsibility.

Then there is the verbal abuse or physical violence on the part of Muslims directed against Christians (very seldom the other way round). Some seminarians told me that people sometimes come up to them in the subway and say, "When are you going to leave our country?" There are frequent violent outbursts between Muslims and Copts.

One example out of many: Some months ago four people were taken to the hospital and thirty-five were arrested following a fight between Muslim and Copt families in the village of Saft Meydum, in the governorate of Beni Suef, south of Cairo. The quarrel broke out after a Muslim girl was hit by a Coptic youth on a bicycle. The girl's relatives stormed toward the cyclist's home, intending to stone it.

Two years after the regime change, things have not improved for Christians. After the momentary appearance of a revolutionary ecumenical dawn, what we now see is a new outbreak of violence against Christians. The appearance and strengthening of Islamic fundamentalists, the Muslim Brotherhood, Salafis, and other such groups have completely changed the political scene and altered the course of events. Many people consider that the revolution has been hijacked.

On Sunday April 7, 2013, Islamic militants attacked the faithful who were coming out of a funeral at St. Mark's Cathedral, hailing down stones and Molotov cocktails on them from the tops of neighboring buildings. The security forces witnessed the attack but did not intervene. Such an attack on a cathedral is unprecedented and very alarming; still more so is the attackers' impunity.

In general Christians are living in a sense of tension or even permanent oppression. One Christian layperson talked of feeling stifled. . . . Another told me at least twenty times, "I'm not scared!" but the emphatic repetitions belied his words.

Speaking of being scared, one sometimes gets the impression that it is the Muslims who are scared of the Christians: scared of contact with them, scared of priests (whom they think are some kind of magicians), scared that their own children might be converted to the Christian God of Love—and so they do everything they can to keep Muslims away from Christians.

So what future is there for the Christians, and what solutions do they see? There is emigration, but it is becoming more and more difficult, with restrictions on visas and a growing inability to meet the cost—people simply cannot afford to move away. There is also conversion to Islam: I was told of a reward for converting of 10,000 Egyptian pounds (1,500 euros), which is a fortune for many Egyptians (a teacher earns 50 euros a month). And, finally, there is the real conversion that is asked of all Christians, which consists of making more room for Christ in one's life. The advantage, if there is one, of the situation of the Egyptian Christians is that they are face-to-face with the essentials and are being ceaselessly called to renew the three virtues of faith, hope, and charity.

The former system of protection is not to be lamented; in those times there was a massive exodus away from the region. But it is true that, when faced with the unknown, there are those who regret the way history has suddenly speeded up. Maybe what is needed is patience; revolutions are complex events. Just take the example of the French Revolution: Thirty-five years after the storming of the Bastille, King Louis XVI's brother was still reigning over France as King Louis XVIII.

The Revolution of Love

Arab spring, Islamic winter . . . which is the next season to be announced by the forecasters? And what will it be like? At this stage it is hard to see what will become of the turmoil that has swept through North Africa, but there is no lack of reasons for hope.

First of all, Egyptian Christians are convinced that God is watching over them and that a special blessing rests on the country where the Holy Family found refuge in their flight from Bethlehem. On the feast day of the Entry of the Lord into Egypt, observed on June 1 in the Coptic calendar, the priests say this prayer: "Be happy and rejoice, O Egypt, and your children and all your lands, for He who loves mankind, He who was before all ages, has come here to you."

Next, relations between Christians themselves are beginning to improve, and the recent election of two new Coptic patriarchs, one for each Church, should enable them to come closer still. Christian unity is more urgently needed than ever, in Egypt and throughout the Middle East and beyond. If the difficult environment and the shrinking of the Christian communities could at least smooth the way towards a rediscovery of unity, then all would not be lost.

According to the new Coptic Catholic patriarch, Ibrahim Isaac Sidrak, elected on January 15, 2013, "The key word is reconciliation—i.e., promoting everything that reflects the peace and love of Christ." In this regard, the patriarch is very hopeful about the new possibilities for cooperation that seem to be opening up with the Coptic Orthodox Church. "The choice of Tawadros as the new patriarch of the Coptic Orthodox is a strong sign the Lord has at last given us, inviting Christians to unite. His first actions, the visits he has made, his spiritual sensitivity, give rise to great hope. We will move from words to deeds, and that will help us to unite in facing the serious situation confronting us," he said.

A further positive point is that the "revolution" is not yet over. The young people, who make up the majority of the population, certainly did not get rid of a military dictatorship to have a theocratic dictatorship imposed on them, despite the real Islamization of Egyptian society. The freedom they aspire to cannot be stifled forever—unless there is an Iran-style lurch into authoritarianism, with the regime maintained only by the constant use of force.

According to Patriarch Sidrak, the negative influences, imported from the Arabian Peninsula and the Gulf countries, "are feared not only by Christians, but plenty of Muslims too. It is comforting to see that very many young people and all sensible people are reacting against all that."

By way of example, he shared what happened to him at Christmas. "This year a certain number of Islamic preachers declared that it was a sin to wish Christians a happy Christmas. I imagined that after that warning no Muslim would come and pay us the traditional goodwill visits. But just the reverse—more of them came than have been coming in the past few years. Groups of young people, families, Islamic associations, kept coming, right up until Midnight Mass. They wanted to show their response in that way."

His predecessor, His Beatitude Patriarch Cardinal Naguib, declared, "The symbols of the old regime have been gotten rid of, but the regime persists. To change it, we need another revolution: the revolution of love."

◆ ◆ ◆

In July 2013 the Muslim Brotherhood were overthrown by an authentic popular uprising. Thirty-three million Egyptians came onto the streets—more than a third of the population (it is as if, for example, twenty-five million French all demonstrated at the same time), to demand President Morsi's resignation. Technically speaking it was the army that actually brought about the regime change, but it is difficult (except for Western bureaucrats worried at this show of people power, maybe afraid that the same might happen to them) not to see the events as the Egyptians themselves taking possession of their own country. At present anything is possible, but most of the population has begun to smile again.

3

Iraq

American helicopters fly low over the town. In the distance, on the horizon, is a row of derricks, punctuated by gigantic flares. We are a little French delegation led by Msgr. Stenger, bishop of Troyes and president of Pax Christi. It is February 2008. We are coming into Kirkuk, one of the biggest cities in Iraq, ownership of which is disputed by Arabs to the south and Kurds to the north. It is a troubled region, obviously, because everyone wants its oil.

Today is Sunday, and the Cathedral of the Sacred Heart is packed. Just one month ago a car bomb exploded by the wall of the cathedral, and today I am struck by the fervor of these parishioners, who put Sunday Mass before any other consideration.

Everyone thanks us for having come in spite of the risk. Even so, we are only going to be here for a few days; they are the ones who are the true witnesses to the Faith. The Mass is beautiful. The Chaldean language of the liturgy is very close to the Aramaic spoken by our Lord.

I can't stop thinking of a Christian farmer we met yesterday at Qaraqosh, near Mosul, in the district of Nineveh. He had been kidnapped and had just been set free after eight days' captivity. He had had to pay a ransom of $60,000 for his freedom, an absolute fortune for a northern Iraqi farmer. His kidnappers had given him a choice: If he and his family converted to Islam he would not have to pay anything. He paid.

As we say the Creed now at Sunday Mass, I think about the profession of faith of that farmer and what it has cost him. "'But you,' asked Jesus, 'who do you say that I am?' Peter answered him, 'You are the Christ'" (Mark 8:29).

Good Friday Every Day

Kidnappings, assassinations, explosions, attacks . . . news from Iraq has been full of all of these for the past ten years. In a mainly Muslim country, most of the victims of these events have been, and still are, Muslims, especially since the "war" between Sunni and Shiite Muslims is particularly ferocious. But proportionally speaking Christians have been by far the main collateral victims of the American intervention in Iraq. The facts speak for themselves: The number of Christians has nose-dived and is now at a crisis point.

Without even mentioning the tens of millions of Chaldeans who were still living in the Middle East three centuries ago, there were still 1.25 million at the end of the 1980s, just before the first Gulf War. Now, it is thought there may be no more than 150,000 left: a 90 percent drop in the community over about twenty years, or one generation.

Another figure: in the past ten years, seventy churches have been attacked, an average of one every two months. The ancient Chaldean community is practically melting away before one's eyes.

Iraq is still connected in my memory with two priests who were martyred at the beginning of the twenty-first century. The first was Fr. Ragheed Aziz Ganni, killed in the courtyard in front of his church as he came out of Mass on Pentecost, June 3, 2007. He had been awarded a grant by ACN that had enabled him to go to Rome to study theology.

He was a young, enthusiastic priest, totally devoted to his parish. We went to pray at his grave with Msgr. Rahho, the Chaldean archbishop of Mosul, and it was one of the most intense points of our trip. Some days after we got back to France, we heard that Archbishop Rahho had been kidnapped. His body was found ten days later, on March 12, 2008, and he was buried provisionally next to Fr. Ganni.

These lives, cut short, are a mystery, even though they are lives that had already been offered up in their entirety. It's a mystery of the cross, a mystery of the Passion, that seems to be relived and prolonged in this country. For the Church in Iraq, every day is like a Good Friday.

Let those who are there speak. The rector of the seminary at Qaraqosh tells us:

> If you take a little of that earth in your hands, lift it to your nose and smell it, you smell the blood of Christians. Iraq has suffered enormously for love of Christ. The Christians have always responded with peace.

Msgr. Sleimann, Latin archbishop of Baghdad, takes up the tale:

> Anyone who has eyes in their head can see that everything is moving towards the disappearance of Iraqi Christianity. The current institutional framework makes sharia the only source of law, with no room for Christians. They

> have the choice between going underground, and going over to Islam.

Cardinal Emmanuel III Delly, then Patriarch of Babylon of the Chaldeans, said:

> At Baghdad and Mosul especially, but also at Kirkuk and Basra, it often happens that armed gangs knock at the door of Christian homes and first force them to pay a large sum of money as a "fine," sometimes oblige the whole family to declare that they have converted to Islam, then force the head of the family to hand over one of his daughters on the spot as a "wife" for one of the gang, and finally order them to leave their house, taking nothing with them, and get out of the country, "because," they say, "it's not your country." Hundreds of families have been forced to emigrate and several dozen families have been forced to convert to Islam. We are suffering because we bear the name of Christians.

According to the present Chaldean archbishop of Mosul, Msgr. Amel Nona:

> Iraqi Islam was never fundamentalist. But after 2003 a radical, fundamentalist type of Islam was propagated all over Iraq. Once in place it was difficult or even impossible to get rid of it. However, the problem is not due to fundamentalism but to the Islamization of society. Iraqi society has changed very greatly. It has become more Islamic and more radical. This is the result of the actions of all these fundamentalist groups and a political method that uses religion to gain its ends. Fear is an essential element in Islamizing society. The greater the fear, the more powerful fundamentalism becomes.

Returning from the Great Trial

Where can there be any reasons for hope in the quagmire that is Iraq? The first thought that comes to my mind is the maxim of Saint Silouane the Athonite: "Keep your soul in hell and do not despair." In the course of history the Church has disappeared from whole regions like the Arabian Peninsula and North Africa. Why should she not disappear from Iraq?

With the Islamic State, the situation has worsened still. Between the fall of Mosul in June 2014 and the conquest of the Plains of Ninevah in the weeks that followed, 1.3 million people, of whom 125,000 were Christians, had to flee as refugees to Kurdistan. What future is there for them? We must help them hold on, but how can we demand that they stay when even their hope has disappeared?

Even today, in spite of all their sufferings, Christians are divided, imprisoned in a "tribal mentality that makes each village want to have its own bishop or its own patriarch," said the new patriarch of Babylon of the Chaldeans, Msgr. Louis Raphael I Sako. And he added, "Like that, Christianity is going to die out."

Despite all of this, we have to believe that Providence will be able to bring good out of all the evil. Even though the numbers have plummeted, it is hard to see how Christianity could vanish altogether in the coming years, even though it is, unfortunately, possible.

Although, ever since Pentecost, the firmness of the Church has not depended on the numbers of Christians but the depth of their faith and their spiritual life, the fact remains that below a certain threshold, the community's ability to practice its faith freely tends to weaken. It is likely that this threshold is not very far off now.

Considering the fact that pride is our biggest danger, we could see the *kenosis* of the Church in Iraq, which can be compared to the *kenosis* of Christ—his stripping, self-emptying, even annihilation—will have the effect of purifying the Church of that danger. But at what price?

Humbler, having nothing to rely on except God himself, Iraqi Christians will find themselves called to deepen their spiritual life, or even called to a real conversion, to greater holiness. How could that fail to yield fruit? How could such faith not become communicative and attract others?

And if, tomorrow, new converts knock at the door of the Church, maybe she will be more prepared to receive them humbly than in the times of her "splendor" when she thought herself strong. . . . She would see in all of this the hand of God's Providence, which is often mysterious, and even incomprehensible.

Who knows whether in the future we, the Christians of the West, may not turn toward our brothers from the East who return from the great trial (see Revelation 7:14), who will become our guides like the first Fathers of the Church, who were also from the East? One thing is certain: The Church in Iraq has not finished bearing witness.

4

SYRIA

Umayyad Mosque in Damascus is, in my opinion, one of the most beautiful mosques in the world. The courtyard is an absolute marvel, and the mosque also possesses a treasure: the skull of St. John the Baptist. Before it was a mosque, it was a church.

At the time of the Muslim conquest, it was quickly established that the church should be shared between Muslims and Christians, because the Muslims were growing rapidly in numbers and needed more places of worship. Soon, however, the inevitable happened: The whole site was transformed into a mosque.

◆ ◆ ◆

When I enter the mosque, two pictures come to mind of two mosques in Morocco. The first is that of the Saudi palace at Anfa, the part of Casablanca where we were living. Unlike most of the Moroccan muezzins, whose call to prayer always sounded very harsh, "our" muezzin—the one at the mosque adjoining our house—sang beautifully. I even enjoyed listening to him.

The second mosque I think of is the one at Setti Fatma, tucked into the Ourika Valley in the heart of the Atlas Mountains. I was with a group on a weeklong walking tour, and we had pitched camp close to the village when torrential rain, quickly followed by a flood from the wadi and landslides, caught us by surprise as we were exploring the village. In the general panic we tried to make for the highest point possible to escape from the streams of water and mud.

We thus found ourselves on the flat roof of the mosque, and we were soon bombarded by a hailstorm, which led us to squeeze into the minaret for shelter. It was a ridiculous situation, but it was the mosque that provided us with a refuge. That day, August 29, 2009, two people were swept away by the river and about fifty cars were damaged or even completely buried under the mud.

Three Keys

To return to Syria, first I want to mention that there is no connection between the Alawites of Syria, who are a Shiite sect, and the Alawi dynasty of Morocco.

Everyone who has visited Syria can testify to the beauty of the country and its warm and welcoming people. Additionally, until the war broke out it was one of the most hospitable countries in the Middle East towards Christians, who made up 8 percent of the population. There were whole villages where Aramaic, the language of Christ, was still spoken, such as in Maaloula—traces of an almost-vanished world, a world that today is at real risk of vanishing completely.

Suddenly it was decided that the Syrian regime needed to end. France fell in docilely with the decision despite the duties incurred by the two countries' shared history: the Protectorate of the beginning of the twentieth century, and France's long tradition, going all the way back to St. Louis, of affording protection to Christians in the East. Admittedly the regime was a dictatorship, but I have yet to hear that we suddenly declared war on all the dictatorships in the world. Admittedly, too, part of the Syrian population really hoped for the overthrow of the regime, and a large part of the armed rebellion—the Free Syrian Army—was composed of actual Syrians.

Nevertheless, as is only too frequent unfortunately in this part of the world, foreign influences have gotten mixed up in the matter, whether as fighters on the ground or financiers outside the danger area. And they seem to have decided unanimously to reshuffle the cards, regardless of the effects on the people of Syria. Three theories, which are also three keys, can help to understand the apparent unanimity (with the exception of Russia and China) of the decision to devastate Syria.

First, there exists an Israeli-American plan to remodel the Near East. To put an end to states that would have the strength to resist the decisions imposed on them, the plan consisted of dismembering those countries, breaking them up into little mono-ethnic or mono-religious regions: a Kurdish province, a Shiite region, an Alawite or Sunni zone. . . .

These microstates would obviously not have the means to maintain their own armies; therefore they would be dependent on the United States for their security. First came Iraq, and now it is Syria's turn.

The second theory is that, in the bitter antagonism between the two main branches of Islam today, Sunnis and Shiites, destroying Syria would mean breaking the broad

Shiite band that arches from Iran all the way to Lebanon with the Hezbollah, passing through Iraq, where the majority of the population is Shiite, and Syria, where the majority of the population is Sunni, but the current regime is in the hands of the Alawis, a Shiite sect.

Largely financed by the Sunni oil kingdoms of the Arabian Peninsula, headed by Saudi Arabia and Qatar, the Syrian rebellion, overwhelmingly composed of Jihadi mercenaries from abroad, would thus enable them to win a decisive stretch of ground in the conflict.

Third, and more prosaically, some theorize it comes down to oil. It seems that Syria's oil reserves were underestimated. According to current reports Syria has approximately two-and-a-half billion barrels, more than any of the neighboring countries except Iraq.

It also appears that Syria's decision not to allow oil pipelines and natural-gas pipelines (running from the Peninsula to the Mediterranean for the sake of the European market) to cross through Syria annoyed the big Western oil companies and, of course, the Arabian oil kingdoms.

By making that decision, doubtless hoping to please its Russian allies, Syria quite simply signed its own death sentence. In this world, it may be okay to be a dictator, but one cannot oppose the oil lords. The United States seems determined to intensify its support for the rebellion, including by supplying it directly with weapons.

For Christians, as for the entirety of the Syrian population, it's a catastrophe. Two hundred thousand are already dead, three million refugees have left the country, and seven million are displaced internally, while food, medication, and fuel are all beginning to run short or are exorbitantly priced.

Increased Faith and Greater Solidarity

Surprisingly, and with the exception of the Alawis, whose very survival is at stake, the chaotic situation caused by the war has not resulted in a heightening of tensions between the different local communities. People have witnessed scenes of solidarity and even protection between Muslims and Christians, when Syrians seem to be putting their shared citizenship before differences in religion. If the present conflict has at least served to strengthen the links between the different communities, Syria will have gained something—but at a terrible price.

There is also a hope that, faced with all these difficulties and seeing their numbers falling, the different Catholic rites will draw closer to each other, and hence there will be greater unity within the Church. That movement is also growing between Catholics and Orthodox, even though their relations in Syria have traditionally been fairly good.

There is evidence, too, of a deepening in the faith on the part of Syrian Christians, as a result of having to face up to the sort of extreme situations that raise essential questions. This renewal of the faith, along with greater unity between Christians, cannot fail to bear fruit for the Church in Syria and throughout the Middle East.

II
PART

Asia

5

PAKISTAN

Quetta, the capital of Balochistan, one of the districts of Pakistan, is quite close to the Afghanistan border. Taliban fighters abound. With the apostolic prefect, Victor Gnanapragasam, a Sri Lankan priest of the Oblates of Mary Immaculate, we are visiting the Salesian school, where ACN provided the money for the priests' living quarters.

The Salesians were robbed at gunpoint two weeks ago. Fr. Cristobal, an Argentinean, spent an hour with a gun held to his head. Traumatized, he has been sent home to Argentina to rest.

We look at the school athletic field. It is surrounded by a wall and barbed wire. It looks like a high-security site. The school is on the edge of a "dangerous" district. Very few Westerners ever come here. In fact, very few Pakistanis do either! The situation is unstable, and the atmosphere is tense.

Half of the Christians Have Left the Country

Balochistan, long neglected by the central government, dreams of independence. Rich in natural resources (natural gas and minerals) and covering 44 percent of Pakistan (approximately the size of Germany), the region is home to a population that retains a tribal mentality and exhibits a growing hostility toward everyone who comes from anywhere else—particularly the many Punjabis (Pakistanis from the Punjab in the middle of the country), who end up moving away, little by little.

To cover this immense province, the apostolic prefect has thirteen priests for thirty thousand widely scattered Catholics. As we look at a map of Balochistan, it feels a bit like playing Monopoly when the prefect launches into explanations. "Here we need to buy some land," he says. "Here we've bought some land, and we need to build. There we need a house for the catechists. There we need a church. There we need a school, which is the only way we can make contact with Muslims and be accepted. Here there are twenty-five families; here there are forty!"

But in the rest of the country, things are no easier. When we go to Sunday Mass at St. Patrick's Cathedral in Karachi, the economic capital of Pakistan, the large church grounds where parishioners could formerly park their cars is now off-limits for security reasons. From experience, people are scared of attacks. Not just anyone can walk in: guards give admittance only to people they recognize. The rector of the seminary tells me, "Half the Christians of Karachi have already left the country!"

Torn apart by corruption, intolerance, and violence, Pakistan is on the verge of imploding. Christians, who make up 2 or 3 percent of the population, try to survive in a country where militant Islamic groups are progressively imposing the rule of their own law. Attacks against Christian communities are frequent, and the anti-blasphemy laws are a permanent threat, hanging over Christians' heads like the sword of Damocles.

The best known case is that of Asia Bibi, a Christian, married with children, who is still in prison, accused of having spoken badly of Mohammed. She was working in the fields when she was attacked by some Muslim women for drinking from the same cup at the village tap as they did. This infuriated them because Christians are considered impure—in a country that calls itself "the land of the pure."

Rescued at the last minute from being lynched on the spot, she was put in prison, and there she waits, not knowing when she may be executed or set free. The international reporting of her case saved her life to begin with, but this fact itself is now working against her. Because she is so well known, an acquittal would immediately provoke large-scale, violent demonstrations.

Mention must also be made of Shahbaz Bhatti, a Christian politician in charge of religious minorities. He was assassinated for his campaign against the anti-blasphemy laws, which are most frequently used abusively for any motive at all, including simply as a way to harm someone against whom you have a grudge.

Some Muslims also find themselves convicted under these laws, but obviously it is people belonging to religious minorities, first and foremost Christians, who are the most affected.

Does all this amount to persecution? On the one hand, one must define one's terms and decide the exact point at which discrimination becomes persecution. Whatever the outcome, the discrimination—if that is the word—has been written into the constitution.

On the other hand there are regular attacks against Christians. Going to Mass, especially at the great feasts of Christmas or Easter, amounts to heroism: There is no guarantee that one will get home alive. Finally, there are all sorts of other problems: the problem of visas for priests, the problem with building churches, the problem of finding work (other than as a road sweeper).

Children of Christian families, which are often very poor, do not tend to go to school because it's too expensive—and there is no assured outcome for Christians anyway. "The priority," someone says, "is not education. The priority is to survive."

A Spanish religious sister tells me: "For the Christian minority here, life is very difficult. Christians suffer here every day, not from lack of food; they get enough to eat, but they are turned out of the factories because they are Christians. It's a terrible situation, impossible to explain."

Regularly this religious sister accompanies families out of the country "under threat because they are Christians." Upset, despite her love for the country, she goes on: "While mosques continue to be built in Europe, here I have seen the crosses fall from all the churches! They want our churches to have plain, flat roofs, without crosses, so that you can't tell they are churches."

Lights in the Tunnel

In certain countries it is hard to find any grounds for hope. For the Christian community in Pakistan, the end of the tunnel of discrimination and violence seems desperately far off. However, I think it is essential to emphasize that not all Pakistanis agree with the violent radicalization of Pakistan society, and some are risking their lives to change things.

How can I fail at this point to offer heartfelt homage to Salman Taseer, the Muslim governor of Punjab, who paid with his life for his opposition to the blasphemy laws, which he said opened the door to the cruelest injustice? One of the Gospel beatitudes applies perfectly to the witness he gave: "Blessed are those who are persecuted for the sake of justice!" (Matthew 5:10). May he rest in peace!

There are others who are working for the same cause in their own ways. Let us hope that little by little, these lines of force, which seem so frail individually, will grow and broaden, enabling Pakistan to avoid the abyss of hatred and destruction.

I will share just one example: In 2009, when a hysterical crowd in Gojra had set fire to the houses of local Christians and was threatening to massacre them as they escaped, many Muslim families generously offered shelter to the Christians despite the risk they were incurring. This is where to look for a future for Pakistan: in the courage shown by some in taking a stand against violence and extremism.

Finally, in Pakistan, too, Christianity attracts people. A bishop told me how one day he was celebrating Mass in a village for a very large congregation, all of whom joined in the prayers and singing. But only three people came to receive Holy Communion, because all the rest were Hindus. They loved Christianity but could not yet take the step of becoming Christians due to social and family pressures. The bishop's conclusion was, "We need to be patient."

6

INDIA

For the past few days I have been traveling with Msgr. George Palliparampil on a visit around his diocese, the Diocese of Miao, in Arunachal Pradesh—an Indian state east of Bangladesh, which surprised me, since I had always thought that Bangladesh was east of India.

We really are in India, even though the Chinese do not agree (on Chinese maps this land is in China). We are at the foot of the Himalayas, close to the source of the Brahmaputra, the other great Indian river. Ensconced between Tibet and Myanmar, the population is Tibeto-Myanmar, though they possess Indian nationality.

Krick and Bourry

During these days, the bishop, a Salesian from Kerala in the south of India (where there is a much higher proportion of Catholics than in the rest of the country), has been talking to me nonstop in his strong Indian accent about "crick-n-boory." I don't have the slightest idea what this is, imagining 1,001 possibilities, including a local make of beer.

Finally I discover that he is talking about two French missionaries from the Paris Foreign Missions Society: Nicolas Krick and Augustin Bourry, who were martyred here in 1854. At that point, they had not made a single convert. Apparent fruitfulness of their mission: absolute zero. Enough to discourage the most intrepid apostle!

And yet, 150 years later, the local Church is in a stage of rapid growth and takes its inspiration from them. It all started in August 1978, when a village chief, Wanglat Lowangcha, who had been to a Catholic school at Shillong, near Bangladesh, had publicly converted. One year later, on August 2, 1979, in the same village (Borduria), 924 people were baptized.

Fourteen years after that, on August 2, 1993, the first permanent church in Arunachal Pradesh was consecrated there in the presence of Mother Teresa. It so happens that the last letter received from the two missionaries was dated July 31. The bishop has no doubt that they were killed on August 2, and that their martyrdom explains this astonishing explosion happening now.

"Christians Are Dynamite"

Founded by St. Thomas the Apostle, the Church in India, with 17 million faithful, has no reason to be envious of France, which has been called "the eldest daughter of the Church." The Church in India is at least as old and now has more practicing Catholics than the Church in France.

Blessed Mother Teresa, foundress of the Missionaries of Charity, is the emblem of the Church in India. The Church there today is fundamentally missionary, with a large number of priests and religious abroad on mission work—so much so that giving material and spiritual support to the Church in India, especially for catechetics and seminaries, is really a way of investing in the universal mission of the whole Church.

In India today there are around 24,000 priests (most of them relatively young), 6,000 religious teaching brothers, and 100,000 religious sisters. Most are highly qualified, with doctorates in theology and Sacred Scripture. The Catholic Church in India includes three different rites: Latin, Syro-Malabar, and Syro-Malankara. This enriches the Church, but it is also inevitably a source of friction.

An Indian priest, who received a grant from ACN, told me that every time he preaches in France, he explains what "Syro-Malabar" is about. He starts by joking that the "Syro" has nothing to do with "syrup" and the "Malabar" is not a kind of chewing gum. He ends up with the statement that if the Christians in India are not *malabar* (i.e., sturdy) by reason of their numbers, they certainly are sturdy in the faith, holding firmly to the practice and teaching of the Church.

This firmness in the faith is all the more necessary because their situation is far from tranquil. While the most violent attacks are concentrated in the north of the country in what is known as the "Hindi Belt," rampant discrimination against Christians has been evident even in the south for the past ten years or so.

This deterioration is basically the result of the political activism of the BJP, the fundamentalist Hindu party in power in many Indian states. The BJP is responsible for the impunity that protects violence committed in the name of *Hindutva*, an ideology of extreme right-wing Hinduism. Apart from actual attacks, there currently is also a movement to pass laws restricting religious freedom and prohibiting conversion—the main idea being to prevent Hindus from converting to any other religion.

These developments cause the Church so much concern that, in 2006, on receiving the new Indian Ambassador to the Vatican, Pope Benedict XVI stated that such attitudes were "contrary to the highest ideals of India's founding fathers."

And, on top of all of this, there is the almost daily violence that takes place against the Christian community. In 2007 (and the situation has not improved since then), thousands of Christians marched through the streets of New Delhi to protest against what they saw as passivity on the part of the federal authorities in the face of violence against Christians in the country. "Violence does not bring peace," and "Let Christians live and serve," proclaimed some of the banners.

At Christmas 2008, the state of Orissa was convulsed by a wave of violence, with five parish churches, forty-eight chapels, six convents, three presbyteries, a minor seminary, and ten other church buildings attacked, and over five hundred houses destroyed. The fact that the attacks were statewide and apparently coordinated, and that the police and army made little or no attempt to intervene, seemed to show that these tragic happenings were not merely spontaneous or unplanned.

Why are Christians treated this way in India? It should first be underlined that the majority of the 1.2 billion Indians have absolutely nothing against Christians; the attacks are the work of a minority of activists, usually Hindu fundamentalists. It seems to me that there are four main reasons.

First, India is currently in a state of rapid change; its confrontation with modernity and globalization engenders tensions. At this stage, it may well seem worth fighting for the return of a fantasized "pure India," totally Hindu, united against the Other, the foreigner, the enemy. In that case a scapegoat would be handy, and Christians make the ideal target, being nonviolent. If, for instance, the Maoist rebels, who pose a real threat to the country's security, were attacked instead, things would be far more complicated: They are armed and extremely violent themselves.

Second, even though Christians are in a tiny minority—totaling 2.3 percent of the population, with Catholics at about 1.5 percent—their presence does not go unnoticed, mainly because of their work in education and charity. The Catholic Church educates no fewer than twenty million students in 25,000 establishments, and runs 25 percent of the hospitals and healthcare centers in the country.

Third, there are continued conversions to Christianity, which necessarily upsets the Hindu fundamentalists, even though most converts are Dalits ("untouchables") and people from tribal communities. The numbers of converts are not negligible, but so far there is no risk of Christianity taking over India. But maybe the extremists are right to feel uneasy.

Fourth, and this is undoubtedly the primary reason, Christianity represents a real threat to the caste system. The Gospel proclaims the equal dignity of every human being, which directly contradicts the principle of castes. Cardinal Telesphore Placidus Toppo, archbishop of Ranchi and at the time president of the Indian Bishops' Conference, went so far as to say that Christians are "dynamite" to the caste system.

With its educational, social, and health programs for those who have no caste, the Church really enables these individuals to change their lives and aim for success. If all the outcasts and tribal groups became Christian, Cardinal Toppo estimates they could grow to 200 million people, and this would pose a threat to the domination of the traditional caste system.

The conflict in Orissa State, which Cardinal Toppo refers to as a "human tsunami," was focused on religion, but the underlying causes were really political and economic. They were connected to the high-interest loans which nationalist organizations made to the poorest in the tribal communities and the Dalits, thus ruining whole families—a useful outcome for those wishing to keep people in slavery. This system of exploitation seems to be widespread in India.

The problem of the castes is even found, unfortunately, within the Church, though real efforts are being made to rectify things. Right up until the twentieth century, all Indian Catholic priests and bishops were from the high castes. It takes time, and conversion sometimes requires a cultural change—and a very demanding one at that.

◆ ◆ ◆

Then there is the problem of women in India. The Catholic Church also upsets sensitivities because of its firm opinions in favor of women. Every seven minutes in India, one woman dies of causes linked to pregnancy, while abortions of female fetuses have reached dramatic proportions.

According to a recent UNICEF report, 71,000 babies are born in India every day, but only 31,000 of them are girls. This deficit of 5,000 girls a day means almost two million fewer girls per year.

In January 2013 the archdiocese of Mumbai (Bombay) launched the 37 Million Diyas ("37 Million Lights") campaign in favor of women in India. Thirty-seven million is the number of women "missing" from India today because of abortions, infanticide, violence, and lack of healthcare. This is the lot of women today in a country whose economic and social development masks the rigidity of its people's mentality.

Having a baby girl means ultimately having to pay out a dowry, and some parents are prepared to go to any lengths today to avoid the issue, including changing the daughter into a son. Indian doctors have been accused of performing sex-change operations on baby girls for parents who wanted a boy in order to improve their family's prospective sources of income.

Ranjana Kumari of the Center for Social Research says, "Operating on girls to turn them into boys, without their informed consent, shows that India is falling into 'social insanity' at a time when the country already has a large imbalance between the sexes because of sex-selective abortions."

Statistics show that the problem is getting worse. "The more educated and wealthy people are, the more they tend to kill girls," Kumari says, denouncing the current wave of female feticide. To combat the rejection of girls, the government should "underline the spiritual wealth that a girl brings to a family, but also support girls and women with financial aid and employment," she adds. The government now seems to be aware of the seriousness of the situation: It has just decided to offer $5,000 to mothers giving birth to girls in the hope that this measure will save the lives of 100,000 girls a year.

"The Church Is Only Just Beginning!"

Let's go back to Arunachal Pradesh. There, as elsewhere in India, and despite all the obstacles outlined above, the Church is growing. However, this was the first Indian state to pass a law banning conversions, back in 1978. "To this day, baptisms are forbidden," says Msgr. John Thomas Kattrukudiyil, bishop of Itanagar.

Nevertheless, today the diocese has around 100,000 Catholics. "The number is increasing," the bishop says, "to such an extent that the Christian vote is something local politicians are keen to attract. In just three or four years from now, every village in my diocese should be in contact with the Church. To achieve that goal I plan to train about 150 new catechists." The diocese of Itanagar, set up in 2003, has a total population of around 660,000. Currently there are fifty diocesan and religious priests caring for the faithful in seventeen parishes.

In Miao, the neighboring diocese, it is the same story: Twenty-five years ago there was not a single Catholic, and today there are more than 50,000. As Msgr. Palliparampil (who has been arrested four times, having worked clandestinely for several years) says, "The Church is only just beginning!"

At Sunday Mass at Lazu, just a few miles from the Myanmar border, the church is packed. The bishop confers almost 300 confirmations and then gives thirty first holy Communions. We are in mountain country, with a mainly tribal population; each tribe has its own culture and traditions, its own dances and costumes, but all receive one and the same Holy Spirit. "In this diocese, there are conversions and baptisms every Sunday," the bishop tells me.

The bishop chose as his motto, "Let your light shine!" (Matthew 5:16), a very natural choice for Arunachal Pradesh, which means "the country of the rising sun." He seems to be winning his bet. The anti-conversion law remains on the statute books, but it becomes a little more of a dead letter with every day that passes. No one could actually put forward a bill to repeal the law, because it would provoke a storm of protest, in particular from the BJP, so people are content to leave things as they are.

The best known saint of the Indian subcontinent is, of course, Blessed Mother Teresa of Calcutta. She was not Indian by birth, although she became an Indian citizen in 1951. The first native-born Indian saint was St. Anna Muttathupadam, a religious sister from Kerala, who was canonized by Pope Benedict XVI in 2007. This is another clear, visible sign of how the Catholic faith has taken root in India.

The papal nuncio, whom I met on my journey to New Delhi, told me that he dreamed of the day when millions of Indians would be baptized in the Ganges . . . The Church in India will surprise us yet!

7

CHINA

Five o'clock in the morning, and outside it is snowing. We are in Tianjin, north China, at the beginning of February, and it is very cold. I am one of a group of students lodging on a university campus quite a long way from the center of town. It is Sunday, I wanted to go to Mass, and Masses are celebrated very early in this country. So I set off alone, all bundled up, hoping to find the Catholic church I had noted the day before in the old town.

After a fifteen-minute walk through the darkness in the neighboring countryside, a one-hour bus ride, and another short walk, I finally arrive at the church. The Mass was far advanced: they were praying the Our Father. The parish was probably managed by the Patriotic Association (i.e., the government-controlled Church), but in view of all the effort I had made and the fact that I had no other possibility of getting to Mass at all, as far as I was concerned, the Mass was valid.

That was in 1990, eight months after the events in Tiananmen Square, and I was in China on a university exchange scheme, studying Chinese. At that time there weren't many foreigners in China, and my presence at Mass was certainly observed.

Thirty-Two Years in Prison

Eighteen years later, however, I am doing my best to go unnoticed: I am going to visit a clandestine priest in his little apartment in Shanghai, where his tiny living room serves as a chapel. There is a little altar, some large pictures of the Blessed Virgin Mary and St. Thérèse of Lisieux, as well as a photograph of St. John Paul II. The ventilator stirs the air gently. I have arrived as discreetly as I could. "Quiet," whispered my Chinese contact as we came into the courtyard.

Fr. Zhu has spent thirty-two years in prison. His crime was remaining faithful to Rome at all costs and so refusing to join the Patriotic Association. "In my family," he tells me reflectively, "between us all, six brothers and sisters, we have been in prison for a total of 146 years."

There is no boasting in this mournful account; you can tell that he has suffered immensely. The *laogai*, or Chinese gulag, is a machine that devours its victims, deliberately trying to break them and indoctrinate them, to put them back on the "right path" by force.

I ask him how it is possible to survive thirty-two years in prison. "I entrusted myself to God and the Blessed Virgin Mary," he replies. "If I had denied my faith, I could have gotten out right away." Every day for thirty-two years, he knew that he could "get out right away" if he chose. When I hear people, even people inside the Church, criticizing the Holy Father, I cannot help thinking of that Chinese priest.

"How Many Divisions Has the Pope?"

China counts for much on the world scene in practically every field, whether demography, diplomacy, or economics—and it also means a lot to the Catholic Church. Even though the results of the Church's investment in China have yet to be felt, there can be no doubt that the Church will continue her efforts, and one day they will bear fruit.

As seen from Beijing, it is as though a dwarf was confronting a giant. What does the Vatican mean to China? A microscopic state, 21,000,000 times smaller than the "Middle Kingdom" (the Chinese name for China—China being the center of the world). How can that pathetic little plot of land in Rome, even smaller than Beijing's Forbidden City, matter to China?

Then there is demography. Here the Vatican does a little better, having 1.18 billion faithful worldwide—but China, with its 1.31 billion citizens, scorns this, too. "How many divisions has the Pope?" jeered Stalin famously. God, three Persons in one Nature, is greater than mathematics, and the Chinese Communist Party leaders are of no more account to him than anyone else; but it is all the same to the Chinese.

Finally, economics: If one added up the financial worth of all the concerns managed by the Catholic Church throughout the world—not just the budget of the Vatican itself—it would come to an astonishingly vast figure. That sum is not capital owned by the Church, nor is she a shareholder; it is at the service of the Church's pastoral mission, and a great part of it is at the service of the poorest, whom the Church looks after.

Financially speaking, though, it remains true that the Catholic Church has sufficient weight in the world to earn the respect of any materialist for whom the ultimate criterion of success is financial. But for the Chinese, the Vatican has a serious handicap: it does not buy anything. Despite its considerable financial standing, the Vatican is not a consumer, and hence not a good client for products "Made in China."

In reality, China, which now has a strong presence throughout the world, is well aware of the Church's action and influence but does not consider that, at the end of the day, she represents anything of significance for China's strategy of economic and political conquest. Does China honestly underestimate the role of the Vatican, or just pretend not to know? The result, in any case, is the same, and that enables China to operate its religious policy, ignoring protests from abroad no matter what their nature.

After all, why should China worry? Nobody stopped it from entering the World Trade Organization or hosting the Olympic Games on the grounds that religious freedom in China was not in a healthy state. One man in white in the Vatican counts for little compared with all the consumers and traders in the world. There is St. Peter's Square, and there are the New York, London, and Tokyo financial centers, among others: China knows which ones matter more.

◆ ◆ ◆

The view from Rome is very different. China has become one of the Vatican's priorities and will surely remain one for the coming century. There are plenty of reasons for this, especially historical ones. But the basic reason is the future and what is at stake if Christianity is to succeed in reaching the heart of China.

Historically China was one of the very first countries in the world to be touched by Christianity. At a conference organized by ACN and EEChO (*Enjeux de l'Étude du Christianisme des*

Origines: "Elements for the study of the origins of Christianity") in November 2012, some speakers, including Pierre Perrier, claimed the Apostle Thomas evangelized a small part of the territory of China between 65 and 68 AD. These claims were backed up by multiple arguments and examples.

After that, the evangelization of China took place in successive waves, from the Nestorians, the thirteenth-century Franciscans, and Matteo Ricci's Jesuits to the nineteenth-century work of the Paris Foreign Missions Society. The greatest missionary effort in terms of volume was carried out in the first half of the twentieth century.

In 1926 the first six Chinese bishops were consecrated at St. Peter's in Rome by Pope Pius XI. Twenty years later, Pope Pius XII divided China into twenty archbishoprics and seventy-nine bishoprics, and created the first Chinese cardinal, Msgr. Tian Gengxin, archbishop of Beijing.

At that time the Church in China had 3.2 million faithful and 5,500 priests, half of whom were Chinese. Then came the rupture under Mao Tse-tung, with the creation in 1952 of the Patriotic Association of Catholics, a national church under government orders. Since then, efforts on the part of the Vatican to mend relations with Beijing have been constant.

On May 27, 2007, Pope Benedict XVI published a "Letter to Chinese Catholics." As far as I know, it is the only country that has been honored with such a missive. What is more, the Holy Father proposed in that letter that May 24 should become an invitation to Catholics all over the world to unite themselves in prayer to the Church in China. This is a completely unique move, and is a wonderful expression of the Church's concern for China. So we are all involved in it together.

There is also a symbolic aspect to the Church's concern for China. Christianity was born in Asia, but paradoxically, it is the continent with fewest Christians today. Apart from the Philippines, where Catholics are in the majority, only in Vietnam and South Korea is even 8 or 10 percent of the population Christian, the percentage being far lower in all other Asian countries. If the biggest and most populous country in Asia decided to open the doors to Christ, it would undoubtedly have repercussions throughout the continent.

For example, Vietnam, despite its territorial quarrels with China, models its religious policy on that of its larger neighbor. The cardinal of Ho Chi Minh City (the former Saigon), Msgr. Jean-Baptiste Pham Minh Mân, whom I met in November 2008, told me it was unlikely that Vietnam would establish diplomatic relations with the Vatican before China did so.

Diplomacy has considerable importance—all the more so because China's economic might is turning it little by little into a giant that cannot be ignored. The Catholic Church is present everywhere in the world, but so, to a growing extent, is China. Normalizing relations between them would benefit both sides—at least in the opinion of the Vatican.

The symbolic aspect also comes into play with regard to China's ideology of militant atheism—which one might think had died in the last century, but still survives in certain totalitarian countries, usually Communist ones. Renouncing an openly anti-religious policy would be a big step towards recognizing the importance of religious freedom, for which the Vatican is actively campaigning.

There is a further element that should not be underestimated, and that concerns the interior discipline of the Church more directly. Since 1952, the Church in China has lived in a bisected state, with one half being the official part which could be termed schismatic, even though the schism has been imposed and instrumentalized from outside, and the other half being the clandestine or underground Church, which, despite everything, chose to keep its union with Rome and has paid (and is still paying) a heavy price for that choice in terms of persecution.

The Vatican's express will is to put an end to this painful situation and enable the Church in China to recover its unity. If for this reason alone, China really is one of the Church's priorities.

Finally consider the demographics: almost one human being in five lives in China. In this gigantic population reservoir, it is quite conceivable that there are some who are capable of listening and responding to the message of Christianity.

Already the number of Catholics in China has quadrupled since Mao's takeover in 1949, which was a time of extraordinarily intense persecution. And today it is clear that a spiritual thirst is developing in a society that has been corrupted by the allure of money and is in search of meaning.

◆ ◆ ◆

What is the situation with regard to persecution in China today? To get a reasonable picture, one must first understand the revolutionary dynamics that gave rise to the People's Republic of China. Thinking back to the French Revolution, there are some clear parallels to be drawn, since the French Revolution generally served as a pattern for the totalitarianisms of the twentieth century, especially with regard to the question of religion.

Apart from the brief interlude of the Cult of Reason in France, which never happened in China, there was in both countries first the creation of a national church to which everyone was required to swear allegiance. The second stage, during the Red Terror and the Cultural Revolution alike, was the total prohibition of all religious belief and practice. Next, the State again authorized the practice of religion, realizing that a legalized religion was easier to control than one that had been driven underground. The final or fourth stage was the reestablishing of relations with the Vatican by means of a concordat in France—a stage that has not yet been reached in China. Napoleon understood that it was in his interest to restore religious peace in France; the Chinese Communist Party has not yet found any benefits it might derive from doing the same.

The 1984 constitution granted the Chinese freedom to embrace a religion provided that it was one of the five recognized by the State: Taoism, Buddhism, Catholicism, Protestantism, and Islam, each with national structures and under government control. The Chinese leadership talk continually about the "spiritual renewal" of society to prevent it from falling into "materialism," but meanwhile they maintain strict surveillance of all religious activities and hence, in practice, they offer a very limited concept of religious freedom.

The authorities also constantly denounce any "connections with foreign forces that interfere in the interior affairs" of China. These "foreign forces" include the Vatican, Muslims (Xinjian), Tibetans (Tibet), and Mongolians (Inner Mongolia). It is interesting to note that in all cases except that of the Vatican, the problematic situation is worsened by territorial questions, which necessarily render any solution more sensitive and complex. Nothing of the kind applies to Catholics, who do not lay claim to any territory or even any special provisions, but only ask to be ordinary citizens not discriminated against because of their religion.

As for the Catholic Church, there are still many bishops and priests in prison. "I have great hopes for the Church in China," declares Fr. Zhong, a member of the clandestine community of Yunnan, "because we have so many martyrs." The ostracizing of the bishops of the underground Church continues even after they die. Everything possible is done to prevent the underground communities from holding a funeral for them. The Patriotic Association makes its bishops take part regularly in conferences, meetings, seminars, and political sessions, during which they are subjected to brainwashing, not to mention all the time lost from their pastoral work.

The national pilgrimage to Sheshan, near Shanghai, the most important shrine of Our Lady in China, has all sorts of obstacles put in its way by the police and armed forces. The situation has gotten even worse since July 7, 2012, the day of the consecration of the new bishop of Shanghai, Msgr. Ma Daquin. After his ordination as bishop, he declared publicly that, because of his new episcopal responsibilities, he could no longer belong to the Patriotic Association, which he resigned from on the spot. In short, he declared war. Since then Msgr. Ma Daquin has been held under house arrest, and his whole diocese has been subjected to an intensive course of "patriotic" remedial teaching and reindoctrination.

The Chinese-language version of the Vatican website was launched on March 19, 2009 (the Feast of St. Joseph), but it is regularly blocked. There are endless conflicts over the question of Church property, with local authorities trying to requisition sites belonging to the Church and reappropriate them for profitable building redevelopment, all in defiance of Chinese law.

Finally, the policy of sowing discord between official and underground Catholics continues without respite. Ordinations are the most visible occasion for this, with bishops pressured to concelebrate with illegitimate bishops who have incurred excommunication *latae sententiae*. Heavily policed, these ceremonies stir up trouble among clergy and faithful.

Ten Thousand Conversions per Day

What lies in the future for Christianity in China? One scenario is that the situation will deteriorate. Faced with growing social tensions and increasingly open demands for freedom, the government will decide on a radical clampdown and use it to take over all organizations, including the Catholic Church, which could well find herself once again banned entirely, as she was under the Cultural Revolution.

The precedent set by Russia, when the action of the Vatican through St. John Paul II played a significant role in the collapse of the system, is still vividly present in the minds of the Chinese Communist Party. Nevertheless it is hard to see how a total ban on the Church could take place these days. In terms of communication the effect would be disastrous, even though the current situation, which is far from ideal, does not provoke any reactions.

The second scenario is that nothing will change. The Chinese government will simply continue to blow hot and cold according to whim, but with the firm objective of keeping control of the Church at all costs.

The Patriotic Association will continue to be involved in the wheels of Church administration and do everything it can to prevent any kind of ties with the Vatican, since on the day that the Catholic Church's situation in China is regulated, it will be dissolved.

In this scenario, the clandestine Church will keep up its fight to remain faithful to Rome, with the risk of ghettoization in spite of the supply of new converts, and the official Church will always to be subject to strong influence from the State, especially in the nomination of bishops who are favorable to the regime, with the concomitant threat of rotting the Church hierarchy from within. Msgr. Savio Hon Tai Fai, secretary to the Congregation for the Evangelization of Peoples, bears witness to this when he says: "The atmosphere is really difficult, and not only because of State control. The other reason is a certain weakness within the Church. One ambitious, career-minded priest may be recognized and nominated by the government. Afterward he will think he can obtain forgiveness from Rome."

The last scenario is that a concordat will be signed, the situation of the Catholic Church finally regulated, and communion with Rome reestablished. Even though in the short term nothing points to any such improvement, there is nothing to stop us hoping for it either. We should not forget that Benedict XVI made solving the question of Rome—Beijing relations one of the duties of his pontificate, and it remains a priority for today's papacy.

◆ ◆ ◆

“If it is Heaven’s will, truth will prevail,” said Confucius. China has its own way of seeing the world and its relations with others. Confronted with mounting interior tensions and centrifugal claims, it aims to clamp down on any sign of autonomy. The Catholic Church does claim autonomy, although she makes it clear that she does not aim for anarchy but always respects the lawful authorities of each country. Besides, even if the Church in China is completely Chinese, she is not forgiven for her foreign origins, especially since her missionaries arrived at the same time as the cannons.

When will the Church in China be able to overcome this double handicap? In the cultural and social disarray of China today, maybe the spiritual thirst on one side and the governmental strategy of restoring morality to society on the other will finally meet together. What has been sown amidst such heavy trials will then be able to grow and flourish, and the fruitfulness of China’s many martyrs will show forth in a real Pentecost.

Right now according to Professor Li, head of the Department of Religious Theory at the Renmin University at Beijing “It is estimated that 10,000 Chinese are converted to Christianity every day. In the future, between now and 2050, China could become the biggest Christian country in the world, with maybe two hundred million believers.”

8

VIETNAM

Hanoi, capital of Vietnam, November 2008. I'm one of twenty-five pilgrims on a study trip in the country. Each day we alternate between prayer (daily Mass, rosary), culture (lectures, meetings with local communities), and tourism. One day we had an appointment with Archbishop Joseph Ngo Quang Kiet.

The atmosphere was rather tense, as the archbishop was more or less under house arrest. He was living with restrictions like all the bishops and clergy of Vietnam, but he was under even closer surveillance because his recent pronouncements had annoyed the authorities—especially those referring to the restoration of Church property that had been confiscated by the government, starting with the site of the Nunciature, which adjoined the archbishop's residence.

The site, which included a large garden, was about to be turned into a supermarket, but this lucrative redevelopment project was finally canceled because of the Church's firm opposition and replaced by a public park as a compromise. The archbishop touched our hearts, because we knew something of the price he was paying for his courage. After our meeting with him, we would be followed more closely ourselves.

Some hours later, as part of our tourism, we spent twenty-four hours on Ha Long Bay, one of the natural wonders of the world, including a night on a beautiful wooden "junk." At dawn we celebrated Mass on the ship, in a mythical setting with the rising sun—an unforgettable moment for all the pilgrims present.

We spent ten days in Vietnam, and we placed each day under the patronage of a different French saint who had been martyred there, listening reverently to an account of their lives before praying for their intercession. The number of martyrs is much higher, but just ten of the French ones have been canonized, all belonging to the Paris Foreign Missions Society. The best known is without a doubt Théphane Vénard, who was martyred on February 2, 1861, at Hanoi.

A year and a half after our visit, the archbishop resigned, although he was only fifty-eight—officially for health reasons but after a long period of conflict with the government. The political tensions to which he was subjected must certainly have aged him prematurely, but some think he paid the price of a diplomatic agreement by finally allowing the Vatican to appoint a representative for Vietnam. In his farewell letter to the diocese of Hanoi, the archbishop recalled that he had lived through "stormy times" when "my life was threatened."

A Church under Surveillance

As in China, the Vietnamese political authorities want to be the ones who decide on the appointment of Catholic bishops, but in Vietnam this is codified by an agreement with the Holy See. When a diocese becomes vacant, Rome presents three candidates, and the Vietnamese authorities exclude the ones that do not suit them.

Here, too, there was an attempt to form a "national church," but since Vietnamese Catholics were far more numerous and certainly more united, the Church managed to escape the trap. With nearly 8 million Catholics, or a little over 8 percent of the country's 92 million inhabitants—an extremely high percentage for Asia—the Catholic Church is indeed strong and vital. And every year there are several thousand adult baptisms and a great number of new religious and monastic vocations.

In spite of years of restrictive quotas (somewhat relaxed today) on the number of men allowed to enter the seminaries, vocations to the priesthood are plentiful and of high quality.

What is more, Vietnamese Catholics are very active in the public sphere, even though they are subjected to strict limitations by the Communist regime, which continues to keep them under strict surveillance. Over the past few years, they have intensified their peaceful activism in the form of vigils, processions, and prayers.

But the international press remains under-informed and virtually silent about all of this, although Catholic activism mobilizes hundreds of thousands of people—far more, for example, than the Buddhist demonstrations in Myanmar a few years ago, which received a great deal of international attention.

A factor that contributes to this silence is the extreme prudence with which the Vatican acts, which stems from a desire to strengthen dialogue with the Vietnamese authorities at the diplomatic level in hopes of giving the Church in Vietnam a wider margin for activity. This dialogue remains in a very precarious state—all the more so because the Vietnamese government looks to Beijing for guidelines on its foreign policy, including its relations with the Vatican.

Meanwhile, there remains the thorny question of the restitution of ecclesiastical property. When North and South Vietnam were reunited under Communist rule in 1975, the Church obtained from the government the guarantee that her properties would not be destroyed and would someday be recovered. This agreement was generally respected until 2007, but from then on the government has increasingly disregarded it, refusing to consider it binding in any way.

Strong economic growth and inflation have favored financial speculation, and the "new rich"—basically Communist Party officials—have gone in for it in a big way. The Church, who has no intention of renouncing her rights, thus finds herself in direct conflict with those in power.

The main reason for the Church's request for the return of her confiscated property is the growth of parish communities. Plenty of parishes, deprived of land and buildings, have nowhere where the faithful can gather for Mass, while numbers of parishioners are on the increase because of the exodus from the countryside into towns, internal migration, and conversions due to mixed marriages.

Some observers consider, however, that these conflicts over property, stirred up by the regime, are really only an excuse for discrediting Catholics and attacking the Church's influence. The powers that be see in the Church a place of freedom—a freedom desired by all Vietnamese, I was told. Because of this the government oppresses the Church through intimidation and violence in order to try and prevent such "contagion" from spreading. Over and above the specific property claims,

Catholics, by fighting for what is theirs, have unintentionally given a breath of fresh air to a highly controlled society that seldom dares to express its rights.

Diplomacy and Evangelization

For the Church in Vietnam, 2010 was a special year that will bear fruit. She celebrated two anniversaries in particular: It was 350 years since the creation of the first two apostolic vicariates in Vietnam and fifty years since Pope Paul VI established a complete ecclesiastical hierarchy for Vietnam on November 24, 1960 (the Feast of the Vietnamese Martyrs).

Pope Benedict XVI had planned to visit Vietnam, but it quickly became clear that this would not be possible; the conditions for a successful papal visit were not in place. However, even the fact that such a visit had been discussed was itself heartening news.

Another reason for hope was the appointment in January 2011 of a nonresident Vatican representative for relations with the Vietnamese government, which was a big step toward establishing full diplomatic relations. At that point a Vatican-Vietnamese joint working group was set up—and this continues to function—with the mission of facilitating contacts and working toward solutions for the various existing problems.

In January 2013 the General Secretary of the Vietnamese Communist Party, Nguyen Phu Trong, accompanied by a ten-member delegation, had a private audience by Benedict XVI. This exceptional meeting could be taken as proof of progress in the dialogue between Hanoi and the Vatican.

Shortly afterward the Vietnamese Bishops' Conference published a letter concerning the overhaul of the country's constitution. "I rejoice," said Cardinal Mân at that point, "to see that the bishops have not taken the road of political struggle and have turned away from confrontation and mutual exclusion."

This unprecedented initiative represented a real contribution by the Church to improving the lives of the Vietnamese in the fields of culture, education, economics, and politics, and it was acclaimed for its positive and constructive approach.

Finally, the Church is not resting on her laurels; a pastoral work of reevangelization is ongoing for two generations of Vietnamese who retain their attachment to religion but not necessarily to the Faith. For two generations, pressure from the government and the atheist influence that permeates education has led to many losing their faith. Some parishes have been left without any faithful at all. Some Catholics have eventually been swayed by Party slogans such as "Wait till you retire before worrying about religion!"

In Hanoi, for instance, no more than 3 percent of the inhabitants are Catholic, far below the national average. Hence there is the need for a huge drive for religious education and Christian instruction by catechists and priests, who need to be well-formed themselves. It is a huge challenge, but it is quite clear that the Church in Vietnam is not hesitant about tackling it.

9

THE PHILIPPINES

Halfway between the well-known islands of Mindanao and Jolo in the southern Philippines, the island of Basilan is a tiny scrap in the Celebes Sea. Bishop Martin Jumoad meets me on the quay of the island's main port, Isabela.

He is frankly somewhat surprised to see me there, not having been confident I would actually get that far. He welcomes me warmly and confides, "I have to tell you something: No one ever comes here!"

I know it is a dangerous spot; Islamic militant groups such as Abu Sayyaf regularly perpetrate attacks and kidnappings. Several months ago, on April 13, 2010, there was a bomb attack on the Cathedral of Isabela, but before my trip I checked with the bishop to make sure it was possible for me to go, and only when he said yes did I accept the invitation.

During my stay on Basilan, everyone I meet, especially the priests and religious, show the same surprise and congratulate me on my bravery (which I soon find decidedly worrying!).

We travel without an escort, as this is the best way of avoiding notice according to Bishop Jumoad, except for one morning when, for a bit of a break, we go across to a small island nearby to bathe.

There follows an epic scene: While we are in the water, about ten Filipino soldiers, weapons in hand, stand in a semicircle on the beach, scanning the surrounding jungle. I am not sure whether we are really safe or in a very dangerous situation indeed.

Seventy-Six Million Faithful

After the attack on his cathedral, the bishop has lived in fear. "I am scared for my life," he says, "and for the lives of the faithful." Isabela was made an apostolic prelature in 1963, and Msgr. Jumoad is its third bishop. His predecessor was threatened with assassination and soon left. Msgr. Jumoad was appointed administrator and then ordained bishop in 2002, and he knew very well what he was letting himself in for when he accepted the care of this church.

In 2007 he received more serious threats than usual, and for three days he had a high fever and laryngitis. Today he says the situation is worsening: "Before, the Islamists were confined to the mountain areas, but now they don't hesitate to come down to the coast."

In spite of everything, he stands firm, holding to his motto "Fides et Spes" ("Faith and hope," or, as it could be rendered, "As Christians we must always keep our hope alive!"). The church at Lamitan, located in the middle of the island, was destroyed by Abu Sayyaf in 2001. It was rebuilt (thanks to funds from ACN) and is now more beautiful than before.

Repairs for the recent damage to the cathedral are estimated at 80,000 euros ($87,000 USD). Our financial support is secured, but just as I am leaving the bishop tells me, "Just the fact that you came has meant an enormous boost for our morale!"

A majority of the population on Basilan Island is Muslim, and 27 percent are Catholic. As on the two neighboring islands, Islamic groups are working patiently but firmly to take control. Their aim is to Islamize the whole southern portion of the country, making it an independent state—or at least a highly autonomous one.

They are the masters of the territory, and they take advantage of this fact to indulge in every kind of trafficking. The Philippine army, however, uses the situation for its own good: The persistence of this hotbed of instability enables the army to maintain high credibility and a budget that is regularly increased.

This trouble spot is no reflection of what is happening in the rest of the country. Mainly Catholic, the Philippines archipelago has by far the largest Catholic population in Asia and the third largest in the world, after Brazil and Mexico.

With 76 million faithful, the Catholic Church in the Philippines has considerable standing and does not hesitate to make her voice heard on the political scene when she considers it necessary, whether over matters of social concern or economics.

After the outstanding figures from the Philippine episcopate, Cardinal Sin and Cardinal Vidal, the youngest in the episcopal college, Cardinal Luis Antonio Tagle, fifty-five, represents a new generation of Filipino bishops. They are responsible for a Church that is still politically vocal but is also seeking focus once more on bearing witness to the faith.

Facing the challenges of political modernization, a partial transition to democracy, and desperately uneven economic growth that poses a serious threat to the environment, the Philippine bishops are determined to make the Church's message more credible.

What that means is a renewed missionary drive among the Philippine population, accompanied by a constant effort to help the Church in Asia and beyond—especially through means of the massive numbers of Filipinos overseas.

ACN has lost count of the numbers of priests, religious brothers and sisters, and lay missionaries who come to the Philippines for training. There is also media work, such as Radio Veritas, a Catholic station also supported by ACN, which is based in Manila and broadcasts to a large part of the continent in seventeen languages, including Chinese, Vietnamese, Urdu, Hindi, Bahasa Indonesia, Russian, and Hmong.

◆ ◆ ◆

This relatively comforting picture should not, however, be allowed to hide a change in the practice of religion that has come about almost unnoticed. Over the past fifteen years, the number of Catholics has slowly but undeniably decreased. In 1997, 88 percent of Filipinos called themselves Catholics. Ten years later the figure was 80 percent.

Part of the problem may be that as a result of its historical preeminence, the Church in the Philippines is to some extent very clerical, in the negative sense of the word. There are still priests who treat their parishioners as pre-adolescents, subjecting them to long homilies week after week without ever touching their hearts or opening their eyes to the clear, compelling message of the gospel. The need for a reevangelization of the Catholics in the Philippines is as pressing as anywhere else, since the average Catholic's understanding of his or her faith may often be insufficient to stand up to the messages received from secular society.

There are other countries in a very similar state. The crisis may have reached them a little later than it reached us in the West, but the collapse may be all the more brutal for that very reason.

A Filipino Pope?

In the conflict between the government and secessionist groups in the south, the crisis currently appears to have been somewhat reduced, and the two sides have agreed a certain number of points. Time will tell whether this is an authentic peace accord or merely a strategic truce, but one can only be grateful for the respite.

In the ceaseless fight against the poverty in which a large part of the population live, the Church's action in the political field and her material help on the ground through a vast number of local initiatives by parishes, communities, and movements give the impression that the Philippines will continue to develop, with an ever clearer sense of social justice.

Toward the middle of the twenty-first century (i.e., less than forty years from now), it is estimated that the Philippines will have the highest Catholic population in the world, overtaking Brazil and Mexico. The Church in the Philippines would thus acquire a certain importance outside Asia, where it already has considerable influence. It could be a model in many domains, including the "old" Christianity of Europe.

In an interview with UCA News on the occasion of the first Asian Mission Congress in 2006, Msgr. Tagle, then bishop of Imus, declared:

> Some people in Europe who worry about the direction of mission in Asia say, "All you do is dialogue." I tell them one

> day you will read our work because this is what is happening in Europe now. The Church is becoming smaller. In Europe they started as a majority. Practically all of Europe was Christian. Now Christians are slowly going down in numbers and other religions are picking up. There will come a time when the Christian community there will be a "small flock," and then they will remember Asia.
>
> And maybe that time they will see how we did mission in Asia. The dynamics may be different because they began big, but here in Asia we began small. They in Europe are becoming small as their society becomes increasingly multireligious, multicultural with people migrating, and there is growing poverty.

This, then, is the responsibility being shouldered by this dynamic, mission-oriented Church that is present and active right now throughout the world. So when will we see a Filipino pope?

III
PART

Africa

10

Congo(s)

Makoua is a little town 327 miles north of Brazzaville, the capital of the Republic of the Congo. Sent by the DCC (*Délégation catholique pour la coopération*, or Catholic Cooperation Delegation), I am teaching French in a minor seminary run by the Community of the Beatitudes. In October 1991 there is a lack of electricity—the generator often breaks down and we use paraffin lamps—and running water is a rarity; we wash in the River Likouala. The telephone hardly ever works.

A Snake and a Sausage

I've been there a week already, and Gabin, one of the young men who attends the seminar, has just been bitten by "a small snake" as he left us after the Vigil of All Saints. He is a very keen catechumen and ready for baptism. There is just time to baptize him before he dies, shortly after being bitten. It is night, the surrounding savannah is anything but quiet, and we can also hear tom-toms in the distance. I think, *I've signed up for two years here!*—and experience a moment of dizziness.

Brazzaville, a year and a half later. Ever since Mitterrand's 1990 speech at La Baule, a certain degree of tension has reigned in the Republic of the Congo. Through that speech, France stressed the need for real progress toward democracy in Africa. In practice it did not change anything very much, but France felt it was better to negotiate once for all—even though it meant negotiating with a long-term (or even permanent) president and canceling interest due on loans in exchange for free access to the country's natural resources (i.e., oil).

Mathematically the largest ethnic group won the presidential elections, and the new president, Pascal Lissouba, is trying to distance himself from France (the Republic of the Congo being a former French colony) by drawing closer to the Americans, who would very much like to rid Central Africa of French influence altogether.

It is not yet civil war, but that is on its way. It will end up in restoring to power the former head of state, Denis Sassou Nguesso. Meanwhile it is common for trees to be cut down to block roads, including in the middle of the city, and we begin to hear automatic gunfire at night.

As I leave the Nunciature, where I have been invited to dinner, the Italian sisters who look after the household administration offer me a sausage, assuring me that they won't miss it; they have just received a large quantity of them from Italy. The secretary of the Nunciature gives me a lift in the nuncio's air-conditioned car, but unfortunately the road has been blocked, and I have to finish my journey on foot.

Sweating—it is very hot, and the atmosphere is rather tense—I conjure up a mental picture of the nunciature's cellar full of sausages and think that the good sisters were a bit mean. If they wanted to receive the "hundredfold," they might have given me one or two more!

◆ ◆ ◆

Gray Gold

At Makoua the current minor seminary houses about forty schoolboys who are considering whether they have a vocation to the priesthood. To feed them we go hunting: antelopes, wild boar, buffalo, and freshwater fish, but we still have to go to Brazzaville for wholesale supplies of sugar, flour, and canned goods.

The journey consists of forty-four miles of track and 329 miles of what is officially a tarred road, but in parts the tar disappeared long since—and so did the road. It's necessary to have a four-wheel drive, and depending on the season of the year it takes approximately ten or twelve hours to reach Brazzaville.

This results in a simple equation: no vehicle equals no minor seminary. The old vehicle has come to the end of its life, and we are overjoyed to receive a brand new one, financed by an organization I have never heard of before, Aid to the Church in Need.

The local bishop, Msgr. Ernest Kombo, put the request through. After being elected president of the National Conference of the Congo, which took charge of the country during the transition from the Marxist dictatorship, he is never without his two bodyguards, including during the Mass that he sometimes celebrates at the seminary, his bodyguards in surplices—but armed.

The recent history of Congo-Brazzaville, whose correct name is the Republic of the Congo, is complicated and full of suffering, but it is practically an oasis of peace compared with its neighbor, Congo-Kinshasa, officially known as the Democratic Republic of the Congo (formerly also known as Zaire).

The two capital cities, Kinshasa and Brazzaville, stand on opposite sides of the Stanley Pool (an arm of the great Congo River endowed with some spectacular waterfalls), but the former Belgian Congo (Congo-Kinshasa) was less fortunate than the former French Congo (Congo-Brazzaville). Congo-Kinshasa was by far bigger and very much richer in natural resources. And in Africa, where there are riches, there are predators.

If you take a map of Africa and superimpose a map of its natural resources and a map of its wars and conflicts, you might be surprised to find that they are virtually identical. Diamonds, gold, oil . . . in this continent always become a curse for the local population. Not only do the inhabitants receive no payment at all for these resources, but they are usually the victims of large-scale massacres, or taken hostage in conflicts between the aforesaid predators: mining companies or neighboring countries, and often both.

Congo-Kinshasa is the most dramatic example of this. This country, which is potentially one of the richest countries in the whole world, has been described as "a geological scandal" because its subsoil contains such rich treasures—including rare minerals such as tantalite, sometimes known as "gray gold," which is an indispensable component of electronic equipment (including our cell phones).

Congo-Kinshasa is also one of the countries that has seen most suffering over these past years. It is estimated that nearly five million people have been killed between the mid-1990s and 2010, and the majority of these killings were in the eastern part of the country, where most of its natural resources are found.

This tragic scandal does not seem to cause very much concern worldwide. I am compelled to conclude that the West must have interests there, because otherwise I imagine the situation would be much more widely spoken of. All the same—five million people killed. . . .

Part of the country, the Kivu, is currently under occupation by Rwanda, a country that mysteriously switched its language from French to English after the regime change. The region of Kivu contains between 60 and 80 percent of the world's reserves of tantalite.

The Church remains the only institution still operating in Kivu, or even in Rwanda, and she continues her pastoral mission without slackening, looking after the poorest of the poor—i.e., the vast majority of the population. The Church does not hesitate to raise her voice and demand the return of a state government based on law, with a basic minimum of security and social justice. And she pays the price for this: Countless priests and religious have been murdered over the years, and countless threats loom over the Church today.

Kinshasa, Sunday, December 5, 2010. The archbishop of Kinshasa, Msgr. Laurent Monsengwo, is conducting a tour of the great stadium from his four-wheel drive. He was ordained a cardinal only two weeks ago in Rome, and he will celebrate his first Mass in red before 80,000 people, including Joseph Kabila, the president of the RD Congo. This is an event of national importance. The name of the stadium—the Martyrs' Stadium—pays indirect homage to the Cardinal, although his outspoken homily today may also make it sound like a premonition.

"Authority is at the service of the common good," he declares. "If authority and power are not concerned first and foremost with the common good and the people, but with their own interests, they are authority and power with no foundation." Thunderous applause follows. "There is no need to kill so many men and women; there is no need for so much unspeakable violence in pursuit of money. It is criminal money!" He goes on to urge "an end to war in the Congo in general, and especially in the east of the country," particularly in North Kivu where violence is intensifying.

But this is not the first time the archbishop has spoken his mind. Some months ago his Easter sermon emphatically and unequivocally denounced the country's bad governance and condemned the ill-treatment of women and children, the generalized violence and insecurity, the financial crimes, the misuse of public funds, and the personality cult of certain leading figures. "We need to identify the anti-values in which our society is immersed to the point of falling into an unspeakable condition," he said then.

On the other side of the river, in Brazzaville, a cardinal was indeed assassinated. This however, was in a different era, when the Marxist dictatorship was being controlled from behind the scenes by the Soviets. Msgr. Émile Biayenda became a Cardinal at age forty-six and murdered four years later in March 1977. The cause for his canonization has been opened.

The Spiritual Lungs of Mankind

If there was one word that summed up Pope Benedict XVI's visit to Benin in November 2011, it was *hope*. Without playing down the difficulties or the extraordinary challenges facing Africans today, the Holy Father issued a clear invitation to change the way we look at the continent, and he insisted prophetically on the "precious treasure" that is Africa for the future of the Church and mankind.

This was Benedict XVI's second visit to Africa, following the one to Angola and Cameroon in March 2009, and it was an undeniable success. His welcome by the people of Benin was astonishing. Msgr. Antoine Ganyé, archbishop of Cotonou, said:

> All the people of Benin, Muslims, followers of traditional religions. . . . all the religions were present along the road to welcome the Pope because everyone wanted his blessing. The Pope's blessing is very, very important for us Africans!

The theme of hope was repeated at every step of the papal visit, and he even shouted at government members and representatives of state institutions in Benin: "Do not deprive your peoples of hope!" Benedict XVI said, "A precious treasure is to be found in the soul of Africa, where I perceive a 'spiritual lung for a humanity that appears to be in a crisis of faith and hope,' on account of the extraordinary human and spiritual riches of its children, its variegated cultures, its soil and subsoil of abundant resources" (*Africae Munus*, no. 13).

The Holy Father's positive statements about Africa pervade the Post-Synodal Apostolic Exhortation *Africae Munus*

("Africa's Commitment"), signed and delivered at Ouidah, the place where the first missionaries arrived in Benin 150 years ago. Benedict XVI wrote the document based on the fifty-seven final propositions of the second Special Synod on Africa held in October 2009.

Africae Munus is linked to *Ecclesia in Africa*, the previous Apostolic Exhortation on Africa published in 1995 following the first Special Synod on Africa and also to the Post-Synodal Apostolic Exhortation *Verbum Domini*, published in 2010 following the General Synod on the Word of God and the *Lineamenta* for the General Synod on the New Evangelization held in 2012. All of this underlines the importance of studying the Word of God and also evangelization, which will be the focus of pastoral activity for the coming decades.

Africae Munus is full of hope:

> "Africa's commitment to the Lord Jesus Christ is a precious treasure" (*AM*, 1) of "exceptional ecclesial vitality and a theological understanding of the Church as God's Family." (*AM*, 3)
>
> "An Africa that moves forward, joyful and alive, makes manifest the praise of God." (*AM*, 15)
>
> "Dear sons and daughters of the Church, especially you, the beloved faithful of Africa, the love of God has blessed you in so many ways and has made you capable of acting as the salt of the earth." (*AM*, 99)
>
> "Africa is the cradle of the Christian contemplative life." (*AM*, 119)

This outpouring of encouragement from the Holy Father goes on:

> There are thus many reasons for hope and gratitude. For example, despite the great pandemics which decimate its population—such as malaria, AIDS, tuberculosis and others—diseases which medical science is still struggling to eliminate once and for all, Africa maintains its *joie de vivre*, celebrating God's gift of life by welcoming children for the increase of the family circle and the human community. I also see grounds for hope in Africa's rich intellectual, cultural and religious heritage. Africa wishes to preserve this, to deepen it and to share it with the world. By doing so, it will make an important and positive contribution. (*AM*, 9)

The pope's Exhortation also spoke to the universal Church: "I call upon the whole Church to look to Africa with faith and hope" (*AM*, 5). But mainly, of course, he addressed the Church in Africa itself. "Once more I say: 'Get up, Church in Africa . . . because you are being called by the heavenly Father, whom your ancestors invoked as Creator even before knowing his merciful closeness revealed in his only-begotten Son, Jesus Christ. Set out on the path of a new evangelization with the courage that comes to you from the Holy Spirit'" (*AM*, 173).

Who outside the Church believes in Africa in this way?

The pope stressed that, although the building up of the social order falls within the field of politics, the Church nevertheless has the duty to form people's consciences to be upright and receptive to the demands of God's justice (see *AM*, 22). The Church has to contribute to building a new Africa, and "to make heard the silent cry of the innocent who suffer persecution, or of peoples whose governments mortgage the present and the future for personal interests" (*AM*, 30).

But Pope Benedict also addressed the bishops directly, reminding them that they are invited to holiness of life, and that their dioceses need to be "models in the conduct of personnel, in transparency and good financial management" (*AM*, 104). He spoke to priests, who should live an exemplary life, celebate and detached from material possessions; to seminarians, whom he called to become apostles to the young; to laypeople, whom he invited to holiness in the middle of the world; and to deacons, consecrated people, and catechists, whose lives of self-giving to God and devotion to their neighbor should be like beacons.

The conclusion of the Exhortation is . . . well, an exhortation:

> May the Catholic Church in Africa always be one of the spiritual lungs of humanity, and become daily an ever greater blessing for the noble African continent and for the entire world. (*AM*, 177)

The DR Congo, or Congo-Kinshasa, has the largest Catholic population in Africa, and the tenth largest in the world. It is also the country with the most potential for development. Between now and the middle of the twenty-first century, it will figure in the very first places in world rankings.

Right now it is the foremost subject of the "hope" spoken of in *Africae Munus*, in spite of all appearances to the contrary. But maybe this paradox is filled with meaning: It is precisely *because* the Church in Africa—and specifically the Church in Congo—is called to such an important mission that it is undergoing such a notable trial.

11

SUDAN(S)

"It was the most beautiful day in my life!" exclaimed Fr. Thomas Iga, rector of the seminary at Khartoum, speaking of January 9, 2011. That was the day of the self-determination referendum, which resulted in a "yes" for the partition of Sudan. When I met him in Khartoum, it was hardly a month after the referendum, and he was still overwhelmed by it all. "At last I was a free man, a complete human being," was his conclusion.

This deep joy, shared by everyone in the South, meant a rebirth of the dignity that had long been denied by the Khartoum regime, for whom the Southerners, who are mainly Christians and animists, were second-class citizens.

It really was a historical moment, and the atmosphere was very special. The country was to be divided five months from that date, and nobody yet knew whether it would work out well—or even if it would actually happen.

Overnight, on July 9, 2011, one quarter of the country's territory (an area greater than the whole of France) was going to be amputated—and with it a quarter of the population, around ten million people. It was all the more unimaginable because the North had oppressed the South for so long.

Khartoum, the capital of the North, stands at the junction of the Blue Nile, which flows from Lake Tana in Ethiopia, and the White Nile in Lake Victoria. The Catholic Cathedral of Khartoum is on the bank of the Nile, just beside a bridge that provides a motorway over the river.

Initially the government had deliberately planned the motorway to pass straight through the site of the Cathedral, which was to be demolished ("Yes, it's a pity, but . . ."). The German contractor, however, refused to do it. Instead of being destroyed, the Cathedral is visible to everyone who drives over the bridge.

Juba, the capital of South Sudan, was still a large village just a short time ago. "It's the Wild West here," people tell me. Apart from some skirmishes on the still partly undefined border between North and South, the war is over, but disarmament is far from complete. A minister was assassinated just a few days ago. It's not safe to go out after nightfall.

UN forces are still everywhere, especially the Russian helicopter pilots I meet around the swimming pool of the Djebel Hotel, who are celebrating their excellent pay.

After fifty traumatic years of war, it will take a little more time before a truly peaceful society can be realized. "Behind every South Sudanese," a diplomat in Juba told me, "there ought to be a psychotherapist for the next ten years."

The Devil's Trilogy

The conflict was an extremely bloody one. Two-and-a-half million dead is the price paid by the South for its freedom, through two civil wars, first from 1956 to 1972, and then from 1983 to 2005, when the peace agreement was finally signed. Added to that are four million refugees, most of who fled to the North, especially the parts around Khartoum. All of this was barely mentioned in the world press.

It is astonishing to realize just how selective we are in our indignation. The tragedy of Darfur was quite rightly chronicled and spotlighted, but after all, there were "only" 200,000 victims. Why were they featured in world headlines and not those of the South, where there were ten times as many? Do some deaths carry more weight than others?

But in the South it was mostly Christians and animists who lost their lives. In the end the realization is that nobody cares about the number of deaths: the only things that count are political and economic concerns.

In the time of Darfur, these interests dictated that pressure should be put on the Khartoum regime because, on the one hand, the trade embargo imposed on Sudan was not being universally observed: China was moving in, especially to manage the oil, in the absence of any competition (particularly from the United States). On the other hand, the planned division of the country was ready to be put into effect, so it was useful to denigrate the regime. In the time of the genocide perpetrated by that same regime against the Christian and animist South, the international situation was different—and the victims suffered as a result.

Msgr. Gassis, bishop of El Obeid until his retirement in 2013, said:

> While the West intervened in Kosovo to help the Albanian Muslims, it did nothing about the massacre of the Christians in my country. Just as Christ was betrayed for thirty piece of silver, the West betrayed and sold the African

> people of the Sudan in exchange for barrels of oil. Once my people have been exterminated, the "Christian" West will happily build monuments in memory of them.

But the fight against South Sudan goes back much further than 1956, the date of the country's independence. In fact the discrimination of the Arab peoples in the northern part of the country against the blacks—or "slaves," as they call them—has gone on for centuries, even though it has intensified during the last fifty years. The North was determined to Arabize and Islamize the South, which was neither Arabic nor Muslim. The refusal of this policy by the South was the first reason for their resistance.

It was the adoption of sharia law as the law of the State of Sudan in 1983 that triggered the South's rebellion. The Church in South Sudan was targeted quite literally—with churches being bombed, especially on Sundays when the local communities gathered for Mass—and her action in the service of the local population was continually impeded.

What this rebellion accomplished was to block the advance of Islam towards the rest of East Africa, since Sudan had been seen as a launchpad for the Islamization of the whole region. It is interesting to realize that the south of Sudan has acted as a barrier in the same way before. In 652, during the very early years of Islam's expansion, the progress of the Muslim warriors was blocked by the existence of Christian kingdoms in Nubia, situated around Khartoum, the present capital of Sudan.

A pact was signed at that time which lasted for six centuries, recognizing the existence of this Christian presence and in practice agreeing not to push the Muslim invasion further.

Then, because of Muslim immigration in the northern regions of the country, mixed marriages, and the growing presence of Muslims in the sphere of economics, the thirteenth century saw the situation reversed, and Islam took control of Sudan. The same strategy continues to be pursued in Africa today.

Today the resistance of South Sudan has prevented sharia law from being imposed on the entire country. Christians count a great deal, even though the new state of South Sudan officially has no religion.

Additionally, even though most South Sudanese politicians are Catholic, clashes between the Church and the government of South Sudan are a distinct possibility, because right from the outset the Church intends to speak up on the abuses of corruption, tribalism, and nepotism, which Fr. Joe Vieira, a Portuguese Comboni missionary, calls "the devil's trilogy." And it is highly likely that this conflict is only just beginning.

Looking at the period between signing the 2005 Peace Agreement and the 2011 referendum, it is clear that tension already existed. Paradoxically the rearmament of the South was made possible by the financial and material support of NGOs and the UN.

The government of South Sudan has not built up the infrastructures the people needed so badly, as it had promised. No schools or hospitals for the civilian population, but heavy investment in the army: new equipment, new recruits.

For Msgr. Taban, the Bishop Emeritus of Torit, the diocese of South Sudan, the situation in the Sudan then was like a "sort of Cold War. In spite of the Peace Agreement, and even though bombs aren't falling on our villages right now, the situation is almost more dangerous, because today the people's needs are invisible. None of the promises have been kept: we are still waiting for wells for water, schools, dispensaries."

In some regions, such as Mount Nuba (possession of which is disputed by North and South Sudan), the people were left to cope however they could, and the Church filled in to the best of her abilities in the absence of the state. "It's our cross," said Bishop Taban. "We are not asking the world to carry our cross, only to be our Simon of Cyrene."

◆ ◆ ◆

The newly created country of South Sudan has some assets: there is oil and water and the land is generally fertile. But presently the newborn country is simply not viable. From the moment it began, it was at the bottom in all international rankings. Ninety percent of the population lives on less than a dollar a day, maternal mortality is the highest in the world, one child in ten dies before the age of five, and there is generalized illiteracy.

Without international financial support and the massive presence of NGOs (there are more than one thousand NGOs in Juba), nothing would work. Even though the government of South Sudan has existed since 2005 and has an army of nearly 300,000 civil servants, everything still has to be created from zero. Pauline, a French worker with a Norwegian charitable organization working in South Sudan, tells me: "There are two worlds: the city, government ministries, the NGOs, the tarred roads—and then there is the village, the jungle trails . . . the real Africa!"

One of the main concerns in South Sudan in particular and Africa in general is tribalism. Juba is not within the territory of the Dinka, the biggest tribe in South Sudan. It is from the Dinka tribe that most of the architects of the victory came, including Garang, the father of South Sudanese independence, and Salva Kirr, the current president of South Sudan.

There is no guarantee, then, that Juba will remain the capital, and several alternative solutions are being considered today. The most probable is Ramciel, a lost little town at present, but one that is already South Sudan's military capital, with the biggest garrison in a brand-new camp built by the South Africans (a sign of solidarity among the different Souths).

For the Church, the changeover is not easy, and she has already made a start with the repatriation to South Sudan of many Southerners who were refugees in the North, many of whom were Christians—so many, in fact, that some parishes in the North have lost more than half their parishioners, and some schools have had to close.

There is a lot of talk about moving establishments—including the seminary and the Sudan Catholic Bishops' Conference (SCBC)—from Khartoum to Juba, but the more the Church abandons the North, the more difficult the situation becomes for the Christians who stay there.

How can the Church handle this reduction in numbers? What room for action will she have in the North when it is almost entirely Muslim and where there are plans for the reimposition of sharia law? There are plenty of causes for concern.

In the South, even though the situation is far better and Christians are not discriminated against, the Church must receive all those who return to swell her numbers, but provision has to be made for accompanying them. The newly returned will have to begin a new life in the most precarious situations.

For example, Joyce, mother of five children, is now living in a village near Juba. Her house (such as it is) is free, but she can't find work to pay for food for her children. She was given some food when she arrived, but now she has to fend for herself. In Khartoum she had to pay rent for her home, but at least she had a paying job.

These difficulties are compounded for the Church by another weakness: priests who have left the priesthood, exhausted by the thankless toil of their ministry and at the same time drawn by the chance of work, especially with NGOs offering unimaginably high salaries that are totally unrelated to local conditions.

More than fifty priests, twenty of whom are from the diocese of Khartoum, have already left, and the same problem is also affecting religious orders. A seminarian at Wau, for example, was recruited by a UN agency. He now earns $10,000 per month. It is no longer possible to find any cooks or drivers: they are all now working for NGOs, with high salaries and undemanding working conditions. What matters is one's connections. But what will happen when the NGOs go?

The challenges that arise—both for the Church and South Sudan society—are huge, and there is a real risk of a general breakdown. "The whole country is one big time bomb," says the diplomat quoted above. In addition the redrawing of Sudan's borders creates a precedent for what may be a larger-scale reorganizing of borders in all of Africa.

A Hundred and One Days to Change History

In spite of these huge challenges, the process of separation came off surprisingly well in general, without the violence or conflicts that had been predicted.

Admittedly, the North's ability to cause harm was restrained by the international context, and South Sudan unanimously decided not to let this historic opportunity escape, but it is also likely that the prayer campaign organized by the Church, asking people to pray and fast on the 101 days before the date of the referendum, also had their effect. The campaign began on September 21, 2000 and finished on January 1, 2001, the Day of Prayer for World Peace (and "Independence Day" in Sudan), one week before the referendum.

What is more, although the oilfields are in the South, the pipeline, refineries, and oil terminals are all located in the North. The two countries have thus realized that they sink or swim together. The remaining tensions are due to the imprecision of the exact border—the contested areas are rich in oil—and by the difficulties of reaching an agreement about the massive income that oil represents.

Building an oil pipeline to export oil via Kenya would be one way of reducing this interdependence in practice, but for the moment it is in the interests of both sides to find a modus vivendi.

For the Church there are also plenty of hopeful signs. To begin with, despite having been discriminated against and made the target of violent attacks since independence, the Church has grown considerably over the past fifty years, from one-and-a-half million faithful to five million—an unparalleled growth rate.

Secondly, the Church has a unique place, especially in the South, and her voice is listened to. And finally, the first African woman to be canonized without being martyred was Sudanese. Born in Darfur, Sudan, Josephine Bakhita was kidnapped as a girl, sold to one African slave merchant after another, and subjected to cruel servitude. Set free by the Italian Consul at Khartoum, she became a Christian and then a religious of the Daughters of Charity at Venice. She spent the rest of her life at Schio, near Vicenza, in the service of the poor.

She died on February 8, 1947, was beatified in 1992, and canonized on October 1, 2000, by St. John Paul II. She is cited as an example by Benedict XVI in his second Encyclical, *Spe Salvi*, which is all about hope.

12

NIGERIA

Our Lady of the Assumption Church, Falomo, in the middle of Lagos, the economic capital city of Nigeria. It is Palm Sunday, and the church is packed. To enter the church grounds, as everywhere in Nigeria, you have to show your credentials, as attacks on churches are everyday occurrences and security measures are essential. We are in Africa; it is a day of festive celebration, but it is also a very special Sunday: We are celebrating Christ the Messiah.

Lagos is one of the biggest cities in Africa, on a par with Cairo and Kinshasa, even though it is hard to arrive at an exact figure for the population. Some say it is 10 million, some say 15 million. It is thought that by 2020 there will be 20 million residents.

The city is chaotic, all the more so because it is built on separate islands on a lagoon. Until 1991 it was the capital of Nigeria, and when you travel around it is not hard to understand the decision to move the seat of government to Abuja, in the center of the country.

As the bird flies, the new, artificially created capital city is 335 miles north of Lagos, but traveling by road takes around ten hours. In Abuja there is much more space, and, at the center of a federation of thirty-six states with 160 million inhabitants, it seems well placed.

Demographically Nigeria is the giant of Africa; according to some forecasts it will be the third most populous country in the world by the middle of the twenty-first century (i.e., in less than forty years), by which time it will consist of nearly 390 million people.

In Abuja, too, one has to be on one's guard. Although it's not a huge metropolis with all the accompanying dangers, in Abuja the risk of attacks and kidnappings is still very high, as it is closer to the north of the country and the instability that reigns there.

A New Front

For the last few years, the worst persecutions of Christians have mainly been in the Middle East. The Christian populations there did all they could to emigrate, fleeing a situation of generalized violence and bitter discrimination. The situation has not yet stabilized, but now a new front has been opened up in Africa, with Nigeria at the center of the target.

From time to time, when the number of people killed becomes newsworthy, it appears in the media, and we have become accustomed to neutral-sounding reports on "inter-community clashes," as though the Muslims and the Christians were equally responsible for the attacks. Clashes there certainly are, but almost always it is the Christians who are the victims.

The cause of the original conflict is not religious, but on the ground the religious dimension is undeniable, since churches are systematically targeted, preferably on big feast days when most people gather there—to the point that just going to Mass is a dangerous thing to do.

People have lost count of the numbers killed and injured, and even the number of churches attacked in Nigeria over these past years. In the northern diocese of Maiduguri, there used to be fifty-two churches. Boko Haram has destroyed fifty of them.

Nevertheless the religious angle of the conflict continues to be minimized, particularly by the Church herself. In part, it is true: The religious factor has not been the main stumbling block. But basically it seems this approach is adopted simply to avoid pouring more fuel onto a fire that is already blazing very fiercely.

The Nigerian bishops are generally at the forefront of this appeasement strategy, especially the best known of them, Cardinal John Onaiyekan, archbishop of Abuja. He invited me to lunch and told me what he feared most of all was the unleashing of a spiral of violence in which Christians, exasperated beyond endurance by the continual attacks, would end up taking revenge. All that would accomplish would be to maintain and increase the violence, dragging the country into a bottomless pit of terror and destruction.

For this reason, with the other Nigerian bishops, he has worked strongly and tirelessly for appeasement. Issuing now an appeal for calm and reconciliation, now a call for inter-religious and inter-ethnic dialogue, now a demand that politicians would face up to their responsibilities in terms of security and development, he has his hands full.

In actual fact the challenges are huge. It is enough to look at the demographics. Whatever the real figures, official sources are always careful to make it clear that there are the same numbers of Christians as Muslims, generally 45 percent of either group in each community. This exact equality sounds very much like a political message. In actual fact, I was told, not only are Christians more numerous, but their numbers are still on the increase, and that this is undoubtedly one of the causes of tension in the country.

However, it is not a matter of exact calculations, and sheer numbers are not the point, because what does quantity matter without quality? Nonetheless the objective reality, which necessarily involves statistics, needs to be discovered as much as possible, if one is to understand any given situation.

Historically in Nigeria statistics are instantly seized on and politicized, and for that very reason they are extremely difficult to establish accurately. Even back in the colonial period, because the apportioning of resources was always made on the basis of numbers, various groups tried to manipulate the data to their own advantage.

But the major challenge is obviously violence. There are many underlying factors. One is historical: When the idea of mixing over 350 ethnicities to form a new modern state called Nigeria was born, the aim was not to create a single people with a single national identity.

The situation in the north had been unstable ever since the nineteenth century, when certain forms of violent jihad made an appearance. Added to this is the fact that education was not equally available throughout the country. A large majority of the young Muslims in the north have received only an Islamic education, leaving them entirely dependent on the Muslim clerics.

This dependence was increased by the fact that Nigeria's economic decline caused growing poverty and discontent, manipulated on a daily basis by politicians whose responsibility for the outcome is evident.

Nigerians—whether Muslims, Christians, or traditional animists—had generally learned to live together, but regularly, and with growing frequency in the past few years, tensions have been stirred up by different factions for their own political advantage.

This fact, coupled with the weakness or even total absence of government, makes the situation much worse. If the political forces in the country united to combat the violence and invest in education, the crisis would instantly be reduced.

But for the moment education is the weak link in Nigeria, and it will certainly not be the Islamists of Boko Haram (meaning "books are forbidden" or "Western education is forbidden") who improve the situation in any way.

Present in Niger, Chad, and Cameroon, Boko Haram is a terrorist group closely linked to Al-Qaida in the Islamic Maghreb (AQIM). Today we see the specter of a pan-African, Islamic arc stretching from Mali to Somalia, with Nigeria as its epicenter.

The most worrying aspect is that Boko Haram seems to enjoy the support of certain religious, political, and military elites in Nigeria's Muslim north, which complicates the whole situation still further. The Nigerian federal government has declared war on this movement, which President Goodluck Jonathan rightly calls a cancer. His name may be prophetic; in any case, one may well wish him good luck in the fight against them, for the good of his country and for the whole of Africa.

But at the end of the day, there is a lurking question as to whether the various authorities really want to end the conflict. The present chaotic situation seems to suit all of them. The government gains enhanced credibility by threatening voters with the specter of an all-consuming conflagration, so that the fearful population takes refuge in the supposed "authority" of the state. The local authorities profit financially from the level of violence. The army is guaranteed a sufficient budget, which can only be raised, never lowered. The Nigerian elites continue to divide up the country's natural resources among themselves, without having to share it with the majority of the population, which is confined to areas of poverty. So the situation suits everyone—except the majority of the population.

Six Hundred Seminarians

In this context of permanent violence and continual attacks, the simple fact that most Christians have resisted the spirit of vengeance is itself good news. It is good news for the country, because revenge attacks against Boko Haram would have plunged Nigeria into a vicious spiral of violence. It is also good news for the Christians themselves, since their self-restraint and maturity shows the depth of their faith.

If Christians resist the temptation to repay violence with violence, it is not because they do not feel the natural desire to. It is only because of their faithfulness to Christ, who teaches them that it is wrong to repay evil with evil, since then evil will win the day.

On the cross, Christ crucified evil and death once and for all, inviting us to forgive one another: "Father, forgive them, for they know not what they do" (Luke 23:34). Forgiveness is the very last thing one naturally feels at such a time. But it is the only way to escape the mortal wound of hatred, and so return to true Life.

A religious sister working in Nigeria explained to me that the Islamists who organized some attacks were "unable to understand the determination of the Christian community to forgive their oppressors. In spite of everything," she went on, "the churches are full; that gives us enormous strength. The Muslims say that Christians must have something special. They say, 'Look what we've done to them, and yet they still keep going to church and don't take their revenge.'"

Another sign of hope is the Church's unanimous commitment to work for peace, and the witness she gives throughout the country. The bishops are listened to and respected by far more people than the country's 25 million Catholics. Their words carry weight, and little by little their efforts, passed on and put into practice at the parish level everywhere, surely will bear the fruit of healing for all of Nigeria.

Finally, the Church in Nigeria has large numbers of high-quality vocations. Quantity and quality do not necessarily go together, but Nigeria has both, and the priests and seminarians generally have a remarkably high level of training and formation.

With regard to seminarians, for instance, there are about ten diocesan seminaries, the largest of which, Bigard, has no fewer than six hundred seminarians; added to these are the religious seminaries of the Spiritans (Congregation of the Holy Spirit), Jesuits, Dominicans, and more. Another example: More than one in five Spiritans around the world today are from Nigeria. This missionary order is now working in many countries around the world.

13
SOUTH AFRICA

On December 8, 2009, I hear that Fr. Louis Blondel, a missionary in South Africa, has just been murdered. It is a terrible shock. The killing of a priest always goes to my heart, but in this case, I had been with him in his parish only ten days earlier.

Diepsloot is one of the townships of Pretoria, the capital of South Africa. It is the kind of place you do not visit by chance, and most people would avoid visiting it at all. Three hundred thousand people live there in the most basic conditions. Picture a shantytown the size of Cardiff.

Fr. Louis Blondel, who originally came from northern France, was seventy. He taught philosophy in Tanzania for fifteen years. In 1987 he came to South Africa, and in June 2009 he had just completed his second term as superior of the Southern African province of the White Fathers, which includes Malawi, Mozambique, and South Africa.

After teaching philosophy at St. Peter's Seminary at Hammanskraal, founding Cordis, an Emmaus Center, and doing development work in Orange Farm (an immense township of Johannesburg), Fr. Blondel had arrived in Diepsloot six months previously and opened a new parish church. He was killed by burglars at point-blank range.

Between Miracle and Disillusionment

Nearly two decades after the end of apartheid, South Africa oscillates between the miraculous and disillusionment. After the first democratic elections were won by Nelson Mandela's ANC (African National Congress) in 1995 and the new constitution installed the multiparty, nonracial democracy the following year, South Africa was a cause of pride for very many Africans—the stuff dreams are made of.

The change from the former brutal regime to democracy was accomplished without bloodshed, largely due to Nelson Mandela's charisma. Nor, however, should we forget the former president, Frederik de Klerk, who took serious personal risks, surviving a series of assassination attempts. They were jointly awarded the Nobel Peace Prize for having put an end to apartheid and laid the foundations for a new democratic South Africa.

This miracle, however, did not spare the country immense difficulties, each seemingly more insoluble than the last. While the country as a whole has become richer, extending its influence to all of southern Africa, vast numbers of people have simply been abandoned to their fate, violence has exploded, and AIDS is killing at least six hundred people a day.

The unemployment rate is around 40 percent—and in some townships may be as high as 80 percent. Eight million South Africans do not have a proper house to live in, 17 percent of schools have no electricity, and a quarter of adults are illiterate. The picture is dire in the extreme.

In a Wild West-type setup, guns are everywhere. Initially for self-defense, the immediate result has been a steep rise in the number of crimes, especially within families. Every year in Johannesburg there are nearly 18,000 murders, or fifty a day; 55,000 rapes, or more than six every hour; and around 280,000 robberies.

Against strong opposition from gun companies, a new law has been introduced restricting the right to carry guns. This represents a victory for the NGOs, which, supported by the Catholic Church, have fought determinedly for this restriction as a way to reduce violence.

Catholics make up 7 percent of the population of South Africa, or a little over 3.5 million. The Catholic Church was very much involved in the implementation of national reconciliation, working with the South African Truth and Reconciliation Commission, which was set up in 1995 to examine the question of human rights between 1960 and 1994.

The final report of this inquiry, published in 2003, identified around 22,000 victims, opening up a path for them to claim compensation. This act of service to the country, along with the exemplary way the work was accomplished, set a standard that was taken as a model by other countries in Africa and even beyond.

The credibility of the Catholic Church increased by the major part she played in the fight against apartheid, even though it was an Anglican archbishop, Desmond Tutu, who headed the Christian opposition. Many Catholic priests and religious were imprisoned, and the building that housed the Catholic Bishops' Conference in Pretoria was attacked in 1988, just one month after St. John Paul II's visit. Part of the building was burned down, and some of their files still bear visible scorch marks.

The South African bishops remain very active in the life of the country. For instance, they encouraged the population to participate in the democratic process, as witnessed by this document from 2004, hardly a decade after the end of apartheid:

> As bishops we urge you: get up, roll up your mats of tiredness and disappointment. Get up and walk forward. Get up and vote. Get up, take an interest in your country. We appeal to you to go out and vote. Your voice must be heard in shaping the future. God has helped us gain our liberation—He wants us to continue this journey through the desert until all of us arrive at green pastures.

The Rainbow

South Africa continues to be a reference point for all Africans. What happens there is of primary importance in the sense that it serves as a witness for the future of the continent. What South Africa succeeds or fails to put into practice in terms of development, the way it reduces or fails to reduce violence, its ability or inability to increase social cohesion and equality—all of these are followed with careful attention by the rest of Africa.

Recognized as one of the famous BRICS group of emerging countries that may well lead the world tomorrow, South Africa still arouses hope for the whole continent—the success of the 2010 football World Cup being an example of this. However, there are still all too many worryingly negative signals, with violence being the most prominent.

Reconciliation with regard to the past has succeeded, and the Church took a leading part in this process. But the construction of the "rainbow nation" is still far from complete. There remains the question of equitable development, with a fairer distribution of the country's riches, and also the problem of ethnic tensions, which are not yet resolved. Like it or not, this is Africa, with all the challenges that are evident throughout the continent.

By her massive investment in education and health and her constant effort toward greater social peace, the Church works day after day to ensure that the "rainbow" is no mere mirage, and she remains one of the key agents for hope in South Africa and throughout the whole continent.

14

MALI

Koulikoro is a port on the banks of the River Niger. The temperature is 42 degrees centigrade. The pervading atmosphere is that of a half-abandoned old colonial town. In the past it was where the railroad from Dakar met the boats coming up from Gao. A meeting point, yes, but also the end of the road. Now it is simply the end of the road.

I meet some Italian soldiers who have just arrived. It is the beginning of April 2013, and the European training force for the Malian army is just being set up. Meanwhile the war in the north continues, and there it is the French who are doing the work. The country was saved, quite simply, by French military intervention in January. All Malians are very grateful, and it is good to be French in Mali right now.

"The Church Almost Disappeared"

The archbishop of Bamako, Msgr. Jean Zerbo, whom I met at his residence, told me plainly that without France's intervention, there would have been no Christians to celebrate Easter this year in Mali. All Malians, most of whom are Muslims, know they just escaped the destruction of their country, but the Christians—who make up 3 or 4 percent of the population—know they just escaped complete destruction. Of course France's primary aim was not to save the Church in Mali, but it was certainly a positive collateral outcome.

As in the Acts of the Apostles, where St. Luke speaks of the first persecutions, the Christians of Mali, says the archbishop, would have had to choose between fleeing the country, denying their faith by forced conversion to Islam, or death.

What they were facing was the end of Christianity in Mali and beyond; Islamist insurgents were planning to move straight into the neighboring countries (Burkina Faso, Ivory Coast, Guinea, and Senegal) in order to prevent any rescue of Mali and also to impose sharia law there.

Like an Eclipse

The dismemberment of Mali began in 2012 when one town after another in northern Mali fell to the Islamist insurgents. Gao was captured on Palm Sunday, and the White Fathers there only just escaped certain death. According to the parish sacristan, who stayed, everything happened in about twenty minutes. There followed several months of occupation by the insurgents, with the radical imposition of sharia law, and the rest of the country could see what it was going to be subjected to.

The archbishop of Bamako then launched a call for prayers for peace, adopting the prayer of St. Francis of Assisi, "Lord, make me an instrument of your peace." The election of Pope Francis in March 2013 was seen as a sign from the Holy Spirit and confirmation that this initiative was what was needed.

In 2012 there was also a coup d'état, ushering in a transition period and the need for a transition president. There was a serious possibility of Archbishop Zerbo being chosen, but he put a stop to this with a blunt refusal. It was nevertheless a resounding tribute to him and to the entire Catholic Church in Mali, which is only a tiny minority of the whole population.

It is clear that the Catholic Church in Mali, which is now 125 years old, having been brought by Spiritan missionaries in 1888, enjoys considerable standing. Historically she has always contributed by setting up and running schools and dispensaries. Many of the people in managerial and executive positions in Mali today were educated in Catholic schools.

◆ ◆ ◆

One hundred twenty-five years later, what is left of the daring and apostolic zeal of those first missionaries? In the villages, "the Church is like a faded flower," I am told. There are few missionaries, the local priests work hard but lack the resources they need to fulfill their mission, and the parishioners receive little instruction in the Christian faith and are seldom visited, so their faith ends up by collapsing. It is not a very encouraging picture.

In the cities, however, the number of Christians is increasing. New parishes are being set up, there are many adult baptisms, and the Christian communities are lively and dynamic. Churches are being built, but more are needed. When Catholics in a given area have no church, they meet in each other's houses, or obtain permission to use a nearby Protestant church. Once they have a Catholic church of their own, people flock to it, the choir starts to function, along with various groups and parish organizations, and the community flourishes.

The Catholics have a special need for all these things, since they are surrounded by such a high number of Muslims. They would like to have a new cathedral at Bamako, since the present one is too small, but this will require a great deal of money. ACN will certainly support the project, which is particularly important because of the present situation in Mali.

When asked whether they would prefer a multipurpose hall, a social center or a church, Malian Catholics answer unanimously, "A church!" The archbishop tells me, "In Germany they are closing and selling off churches. I've said to them, 'Give me the money from the sale of your church and I can build my cathedral!'"

We in the West may find all this hard to take in, since we have a huge number of churches and stress is laid on the horizontal, social dimension of the Church's mission. The archbishop continues:

> A European missionary was leaving after spending his whole life working here in Mali, and I invited him to dinner to mark the occasion. He told me he was against building a new cathedral, as he thought it would be better to look after the poor instead. But Catholics in Mali want churches; they want visibility. They want to come out of the catacombs. A cathedral would give Catholics renewed courage. The former president donated a large piece of ground for it, saying, "People need to see a church so they understand that this country is not confined to Muslims." In Europe right now there is like an eclipse, but the Faith will return! You shouldn't sell off the churches, because if you do, in fifty years' time people will reproach your memory for it.

May God hear his words!

♦ ♦ ♦

In Mali, fetishism is widespread. People distinguish between "God," whom they see as the supreme being but somewhat inaccessible to them, and the spirits whom they have to deal with. They would like to be freed from them, and Christianity is able to offer them that freedom, but meanwhile they feel that they have to live, even though it is a life of fear. Everyone has a *gri-gri*, or talisman, which is supposed to offer protection but at the same time holds them captive.

The question is how to show them that Christianity means true liberation from that captivity, not an additional enslavement. Little by little, in the cities, with the advent of modernity, people are turning away from such practices.

It is also noticeable that second- and third-generation Catholics are finally free from the fetishism that dogged their forebears. It will take time—but after all, the very first generations of Christians in Europe probably were not very much more emancipated than Malians either.

Faith More Precious Than Gold

In the south, a mirage of gold glows. Near Yanfolila, a prefecture not far from Guinea, the parish priest of Goualala takes me to visit a gold mine near the village of Rourou. Rather than a true mine, it is basically a large number of holes in the hillside that give access to hastily built galleries that allow Malians to dig through the earth in the hopes of striking a vein of gold—or even a gold nugget.

Will gold ever save the country? Meanwhile it certainly disrupts the local population. Everyone rushes to find it, and laborers for any other work are impossible to find. Even students abandon their studies in the hope of making a fortune. What will be left once the gold rush disappears?

Above all, how will Mali ever manage to enable the much more important mirage of unity and social cohesion between north and south to become a reality? Only the future can tell, but the Church has a clear role to play in this transformation. Recognized and respected for her social work and contribution to peace, she could attract a certain number of Malians who have been appalled by the violence of the Islamists. For the time being, she continues calmly on her way, growing larger, with communities that are dynamic and proud of their faith.

In his first letter, St. Peter exhorts us:

> You rejoice, though now for a little while you may have to suffer various trials, so that the genuineness of your faith, more precious than gold which though perishable is tested by fire, may redound to praise and glory and honor at the revelation of Jesus Christ. (1 Peter 1:6–7)

IV
Part

Latin America

15

BRAZIL

Corcovado. Overlooking the bay of Rio de Janeiro, the 125-foot statue of Christ the Redeemer seems to embrace with outstretched arms the whole city, all of Brazil, and even the entire South American continent. The magical view reaches from Sugarloaf Mountain to Copacabana and even, a little further to the right, to Ipanema, the city's other fabled beach.

But behind the picture-postcard appearance lies a different world, a world of destitution, poverty, and violence—the world of the *favelas* or shantytowns. Brazil means "carnival," but it also means a million violent deaths in the past thirty years—a figure comparable to a country at war.

There are multiple factors underlying the violence: the lack of will on the part of politicians to find lasting solutions instead of vote-catching measures; the feebleness of efforts at prevention; the ineffectiveness of the fight against crime; and above all the culture of impunity, since just .03 percent of murders are followed up by the justice system.

Without being more dangerous than other places in Brazil, living in Rio de Janeiro requires a reasonable degree of alertness. I am here to visit ACN's Brazilian office, which is in

Sao Paulo but has a branch in Rio. They use the same communication methods as the rest of the Brazilian people, and by employing television and telephone in innovative ways they are showing progress year after year.

At the foot of the statue of Christ the Redeemer, I call to mind the prayer offered by Fr. Werenfried von Straaten, founder of ACN, on this same spot some fifty years earlier:

> Lord Jesus, I come from afar to speak to you in the name of the poor. Allow me to tell you: What I have seen in this continent is a scandal. The situations prevailing here are a crying shame for the whole of Christianity. I know very well, Lord, that it is not you who are to blame for this. It is we who are to blame. Here on this mountain is only your statue, a Christ of stone, hauled up here by mules in separate pieces. The living Christ is us, it is what we have to be.

Why So Much Erosion?

Brazil is the fifth largest country in the world in both area and population, and it is already one of the world's economic giants, pursuing a sustained path of development.

The situation of the Church is quite special. Out of 194 million inhabitants, there are 128 million Catholics—two-thirds of the population—making Brazil the most Catholic country in the world in terms of numbers. The Brazilian episcopate is also the largest in the world, with 417 bishops and 38 archbishops. The Catholic Church in Brazil has 268 dioceses, archdioceses, and prelatures.

Until the 1970s Catholicism was not only the religion of the vast majority of Brazilians but almost the only religion in the country. The 1980 census for the first time showed the proportion of Catholics stood at just under 90 percent. Ten years later, 83 percent of Brazilians were Catholics. After another decade, the percentage had dropped again, to 74 percent.

Today only 66 percent of Brazilians are Catholics, so the last thirty or forty years have shown a steady reduction. During this time there has been a process of religious diversification with the development of Evangelical churches, whether traditional or Pentecostal, and growing numbers of people who declare themselves to have no religion. Other religions—spiritism, *umbanda*, oriental religions, Judaism, and Islam—have stood at around 3 percent of the population since 1980.

There are many complex reasons for the decline in numbers of Catholics. It is usually explained by general cultural changes—modernization, secularization, individualism, subjectivism, relativism, and hedonism—but these things affect all religions equally.

Two main factors seem to have been at work. On the one hand, linked to demographic growth, there have been large migrations within country, and people have lost their habitual framework of reference in the process. Secondly, the Church was unable to provide a sufficient response to the needs of such masses of people arriving in recently developing areas or the peripheries of the big cities.

In short, the institutional provision was inadequate, and the availability of pastoral resources, even in terms of priests alone, was completely insufficient. In a way it can be said that it was not so much that the faithful left the Church, but the Church was unable to stay with the faithful in the way that was needed.

It may seem paradoxical, but the Catholic Church in Brazil is desperately short of human and financial resources to serve the Catholic faithful adequately. You cannot create a priest by clicking your fingers or fabricate one in three months. At the end of the day, in order to supply much-needed pastoral resources, money is the basic weapon, here as elsewhere. This is why Brazil remains one of the foremost recipients of support from ACN.

For Evangelicals and other religious groups, including some large sects, much larger sources of income often come from the USA—or sometimes from doubtful origin: money laundering the proceeds of drug-smuggling. Additionally the training of a pastor or local group leader is usually a much quicker process, and it is certainly much easier to recruit them than it is to nurture vocations to the Catholic priesthood.

The Catholic Church is once again faced with vast parishes and the premature exhaustion of the priests' physical and spiritual strength. When the priest has to take care of several thousand practicing Catholics, simply administering the sacraments can easily take up every moment of his time, leaving him neither time nor energy to devote to proper pastoral duties. As a result Catholics migrate to other churches.

With more priests and more resources that would enable new parishes to be set up, the downward curve could soon be reversed. There are plenty of examples of places where a parish has opened and suddenly large numbers of people returned to the Catholic Church.

In the end the picture is fairly simple. Nature abhors a vacuum, and in the absence of the Catholic Church, Brazilians, who are naturally religious, seek elsewhere for something to quench their spiritual thirst.

A New Song

Reasons for hope, nevertheless, are not lacking. First, the Catholic Church is respected for the services she provides to Brazilian society. She is very committed to social work and has set up a whole battery of "social pastoral works" to tend society's sorest needs in the areas of health, prisoners, marginalized women, migrants, and children.

Most well known of all is the Church's pastoral work regarding questions of land, even though her work here is liable to be hijacked by politicians. The Church contributes strongly to the defense of peasants who have no land, whether they have never owned any or have been dispossessed.

Secondly, at the same time the Church stresses the importance of social development, various spiritual currents or movements have also arisen within the Church. The Charismatic Renewal movement, for instance, has taken strong root, renewing parishes and offering prayer groups for those who wish to take part.

There are now several hundred different Catholic communities and associations, each having a strong vocational and missionary drive. This has definitely helped stem the flow of Catholics drawn by the emotional appeal of Evangelical churches.

The Church has, additionally, invested in the media, with dynamic Catholic radio stations and television channels broadcasting across this immense country, even though they lack the wealth of resources of their Protestant and Evangelical competitors.

Finally, the Church in Brazil is a young Church, endowed with strong missionary potential. She currently has 1,600 missionaries working abroad, including 600 in Africa, forty-nine in North America, and 331 in Europe—such as in France, with *Cançao Nova* (New Song), *Shalom*, and *Nova Aliança*. So the largest Catholic country in the world is coming to wake up the "eldest daughter of the Church"!

16

COLOMBIA

Cali is the second largest city in Colombia. After Bogota, the capital, perched at a height of six-and-a-half feet above sea level, Cali's tropical atmosphere, three feet lower, is something one appreciates. Cali is the Colombian capital of salsa, I learn when I arrive, but here as elsewhere in the country, the exciting party appearance cannot mask the reigning atmosphere of extreme violence.

Measured by the number of Catholics, Colombia is ranked seventh in the world. At the same time, it is one of the most dangerous countries in the world due to drug-trafficking, atrocities by various paramilitary groups, and a culture of violence that has developed over the past half-century and fostered by the extreme poverty of so many of the population.

Only 125 Murders

It is the beginning of July 2011, and Cali municipal authorities are feeling pleased: There were only 125 murders in the city in June, which is thirty-nine fewer than the month before. A reduction of 24 percent is not negligible, even though something over four murders every day is still a distinctly alarming figure.

The figures are about the same for Colombia's other two biggest cities, Bogota and Medellin (notorious for being at the heart of the drug trade), even though the situation is less dire than a few years ago.

Priests as Targets

At the beginning of Holy Week 2011, Pope Benedict XVI called for peace and an end to violence in Colombia. Uniting himself to the Day of Prayer for the Victims of Violence held on Good Friday, the pope urgently called Colombians "to conversion, repentance, and reconciliation," and cried out: "Enough of violence in Colombia! May she live in peace!"

This Day of Prayer was the initiative of the Colombian Bishops' Conference, whose secretary, Msgr. Juan Vicente Cordoba Villota, auxiliary bishop of Bucaramanga, presented the challenge: "I invite all Catholics and all Colombians of good will to meditate deeply on suffering and the reality of the victims of violence," and added, "I ask the members of parliament to listen to the voice of the people of Colombia, that they might govern with social responsibility and work in favor of the victims."

The bishop went on: "The Church does not offer specific technical solutions or support any particular political party, but she closely follows the legislative process and continues to work so that the rights of the poorest and weakest citizens might be recognized and effectively protected." He concluded: "Violence in different forms has been a constant feature of our nation's political and social history. There have been a huge number of victims, but for the most part, they remain invisible and forgotten."

The Day of Prayer aimed to be a way of showing Colombians' solidarity toward the victims, "accompanying them on their path of reconciliation and forgiveness."

Even though the Colombian army has reconquered certain parts of the country in recent years, the violations of human rights and virtually total impunity all persist in Colombia. At the beginning of June 2011, to mark the 300th day of the presidency of Juan Manuel Santos, many European organizations made their voices heard, demanding that their governments put more effective pressure on Bogota.

A document was drawn up, signed, and presented, giving facts and figures and saying, "Fine words do nothing to halt the violation of human rights in Colombia." Between July 2010 and April 2011, there had been 206 separate known attacks against defenders of human rights, including thirty-four murders. Fifteen peasant leaders who were campaigning for land for their communities had also been murdered. There had been 230 known cases of attacks on trades unionists, including twenty-four murders. Additionally 122 Colombian Indian leaders had also been murdered.

In the first four months of 2010 alone, over 36,000 people had been forcibly driven from their homes. A project is afoot to restore two million hectares of land to these displaced peasants, but the total amount of land stolen is six million hectares. What about the remaining four million?

With regard to impunity—which according to the International Office on Human Rights (Action Colombia) approaches 97 percent of cases brought against over 50,000 demobilized paramilitaries—in the context of the process opened by the "Justice and Peace" Law 975 promulgated in 2005, the Supreme Court of Justice has only handed down one firm conviction.

Another example: Between 2001 and 2009, 490,000 women have been victims of sexual attacks. Out of 70,780 crimes confessed by the paramilitaries, only sixty-nine cases referred explicitly to sexual crimes, but presently no sentence has been handed down against this type of crime.

In this context the Church aims to increase support for the victims of the paramilitaries. In a piece published on April 26, 2011, Msgr. Julio Cesar Vidal Ortiz, bishop of Monteria, in north Colombia, condemned the government's inaction against illegal armed groups and stated that the Church should take the initiative by contacting international organizations like the Red Cross, the United Nations, or the Organization of American States.

Another great challenge is the scourge of child soldiers, of whom there are nearly 11,000 in Colombia. A note from the Brazilian press agency ADITAL suggests that this figure should be increased by adding the number of children used as "land mine detectors" by the armies so that the soldiers themselves can move forward unhindered.

The paramilitary groups and guerilla fighters continue to attract children by trickery or simply kidnap them, and they sometimes even organize recruitment drives in schools.

◆ ◆ ◆

Whether because of the commitment to work for justice and peace or simply by being at the service of the poorest in the most dangerous areas, the Church often pays the price, especially through priests who are especially targeted: Colombia holds the unenviable world record for numbers of murdered priests. By way of illustration, here are just two examples of priests killed in the first half of 2011.

Fr. Luis Carlos Orozco Cardona, twenty-six years old and vicar-priest of the cathedral, was killed by a minor at Rio Negro, Antioquia, on the evening of February 12. The motive for the murder remains unknown.

"We are deeply concerned at the foul murder of Fr. Luis Carlos Orozco Cardona," runs the communiqué signed by the bishop and his clergy. "It shows once again the serious crisis of human and Christian values that our society is suffering from because people have forgotten God and despise human life and the dignity of the human person."

On May 12 it was Fr. Gustavo Garcia's turn. Thirty-four years old, he was a priest of the Congregation of Jesus and Mary. He was waiting for a bus in Calle 68, Bogota, on his way to visit the sick, when a criminal attacked him with a knife in an attempt to steal his cell phone. He later died of his injuries.

Overall great care has to be taken, especially in those difficult districts where priests, despite the danger, continue to carry out their pastoral work for the destitute. In general they can anticipate and sense danger, but they are never safe from serious harm.

Clearly, some attacks are not the result of any kind of discrimination, but simply violent crime. The fact remains, however, that it is because of the Church's faithfulness to her mission of serving the poorest people in the worst districts that these kinds of tragedy can occur. If the priests remained within the affluent districts, the price to be paid would not be the same. But then, nor would their configuration with Christ.

"The Church Has an Irreplaceable Role"

None of this prevents the Church from carrying out a real service to ordinary people, including social work. Even the Colombian government often channels food aid through the parishes, knowing that the Catholic Church alone possesses the networks and competence needed for tending the people most in need.

Angelino Garzon, the vice president of Colombia, who I met in Bogota, says, "The Church has an irreplaceable role," both in social work, where he acknowledged her "very great effectiveness," and for the process of reconciliation in the country.

The Church has a notable position in Colombian society. She has founded schools, hospitals, health centers, and universities—and Colombians do not forget any of that. They also know that the Church is the only organization officially authorized to negotiate with the FARC (Armed Revolutionary Forces of Colombia), a large and very violent terrorist organization, and other armed groups.

In addition, it is a young Church. The average age of priests in Colombia is under fifty, with some dioceses, such as Barranquilla, where it is thirty-eight. The number of priests is increasing. Religious orders are flourishing, especially the Dominicans and apostolic orders with very specific congregations—for example, a community of religious sisters dedicated to the education and evangelization of the indigenous tribes living in the Colombian jungle.

With 87 percent of the population calling themselves Catholic, it is apparent that Colombian society is still deeply Christian. World Youth Day in Madrid in 2011 saw 5,000 Colombians make the trip, which is remarkable considering the length of the journey and the standard of living in Colombia.

There are two Colombian communities in the diocese of Frejus-Toulon, in France: the Missionaries of Christ the Teacher and the Community of the Immaculate Conception. Colombia, too, is evangelizing Europe.

17

NICARAGUA

Managua, capital of Nicaragua, was practically wiped off the map by earthquakes in 1885, 1931, and finally 1972, on December 23rd when 10,000 people were killed and 500,000 made homeless. The city has never really recovered. The new city has been built beside the old one in a fairly haphazard way.

The cathedral was badly damaged, the roof collapsed, but the huge edifice still retains some traces of its past glory. Today, reduced to a sort of ghost ship in the deserted port, it stands as the symbol of this dead city.

♦ ♦ ♦

When I visited the ruins of the cathedral and city, I could not help thinking of Japan, where I had been ten months earlier. I was with Regis Anouil, chief editor of *Eglises d'Asie*, the Paris Foreign Missions Society information service, and at the end of our stay in the Japanese islands, we came to Nagasaki, the historical heart of Japanese Christianity. Founded by St. Francis Xavier on August 15, 1549, the Church in Japan soon underwent violent persecution and disappeared—at least from official view.

In reality, Christian families kept the flame alive in absolute secrecy and without any sacramental support for three centuries. To the astonishment of the first Paris Foreign Missionaries to arrive there in 1860, they discovered Christian communities that had maintained their fidelity to the Faith for all those years.

On the day before we were to return to France, March 11, 2011, we were just finishing a series of meetings in Tokyo when suddenly, in the heart of that metropolis of 30 million inhabitants, the ground began to shake.

At first we were delighted to experience an earthquake, the first in our ten days there, but we soon changed our minds for several reasons: the quake was an extremely strong one (magnitude 9, but fortunately for us the epicenter was almost 250 miles from Tokyo), then because it seemed to go on and on, and finally because even the Japanese seemed panic-stricken.

The skyscrapers around us were visibly swaying, and we could see hanging lights on the first floor swinging round like the blades of an electric fan. Everyone rushed to the center of the huge crossroads where we were, people got out of their cars . . . and all we could do was wait.

In the end we were all right, but getting back to the Paris Foreign Missions house and then getting to the airport the next day was like running an obstacle course. Nothing was working, both underground and above ground trains had stopped running, taxis were unavailable at any price, and aftershocks continued throughout the night, not subsiding until we reached the airport. It was some hours before we learned about the tragedy of the tsunami and the accident to Fukushima nuclear power station.

Back to Managua: At the beginning of the twentieth century, Nicaragua was the richest country in Central America. Now it is the poorest country in all of Latin America except for Haiti, and earthquakes are not the only reason. Paradoxically it is also the safest country in Central America, proving that there is no automatic poverty to violence ratio. Having said that, the police are everywhere; this might be an example of cause and effect.

It is also true that comparisons between the countries of Central America may not mean much, as it is one of the most dangerous regions on earth, with a mind-boggling rate of homicides. For instance, with 91.6 homicides per 100,000 inhabitants, the risk of dying a violent death is 130 times higher in Honduras than in France, where the official rate is 0.7 per 100,000.

Central America: Civil Wars and Drug-Traffickers

Central America is an isthmus linking the north and south halves of the continent. It includes seven countries, which all have a number of points in common. The majority of the people in each country are Catholics, but few of them practice their faith, and there is now much competition from various religious sects. Almost all of the countries have recently emerged from civil wars and today are still immersed in an atmosphere of violence, drug-traffickers, and widespread poverty.

In Panama the Church is the institution with the most credibility, but there are not enough priests to accommodate the few practicing Catholics. The country's economic growth, fed by revenue from the Panama Canal and a large investment in construction, has left Panama a prey to rapid secularization, but the apparently vast riches are owned by a minority.

In this Central American version of Dubai, the Church carries out pastoral work of evangelization and the nurturing of vocations, which is beginning to bear fruit. On January 12, 2013, the diocese of Panama, the first diocese on the mainland of the American continent, celebrated its 500th anniversary.

Costa Rica is, together with Panama, the only fairly calm country in the region, with a lower rate of violence than its western neighbors, though that is changing little by little as drug-traffickers arrive and establish their territories. A distinguishing feature of Costa Rica is that it has no army; it was dissolved in 1948 to put an end to a succession of military coups. Tourism is an important source of income, mainly on the coasts—the Pacific to the south and the Atlantic and Caribbean to the north.

The Church in Costa Rica does not currently face major difficulties. At Cartago, near San Jose, the capital, is a shrine of Our Lady called *La Negrita,* and on August 2 every year there is a two-million-strong pilgrimage there from Costa Rica itself and neighboring countries.

In Nicaragua the Church has legitimacy and credibility, even though the sects, which are a profitable type of commercial activity, are proliferating. For the last ten years, the Church has undertaken a missionary outreach that is beginning to yield fruit. However, underlying tensions remain between the Church and the government, which gives financial help only subject to conditions that restrict the Church's freedom of speech. Today the country is run by Ortega, a former Sandinista who was reelected in 2011, but massive frauds and the simmering conflict with the Church impelled the bishops to boycott his investiture ceremony.

Msgr. Mata Guevara, bishop of Esteli (the third largest city in the country) was often employed as a mediator in the time of the civil war in Nicaragua. He is widely listened to in the country. His diocese is in the north of Nicaragua, reaching as far as the border with Honduras. This is the homeland of the Contras rebel groups; Bishop Guevara thinks that war could break out again.

The army and police are once again actively on the offensive against anti-Sandinista elements. The Contras are again armed, with weapons from Honduras and probably support from the USA. At the same time the anti-government militants in Honduras receive weapons from the Nicaraguan army—a fair exchange.

Twenty years after the peace accords were signed on January 16, 1992, El Salvador is not liable to risk another civil war in the short term, but violence is still a dramatic scourge, especially because of the Maras, gangs indulging in extreme violence. After the peace accord the USA repatriated many Salvadorians who had sought refuge in the States, but some of them did not find work and were unwilling to be reintegrated into the poverty-stricken Salvadorian society—and instead turned to crime.

The Church is still deeply scarred by the bloodshed of the 1980s, a decade which saw huge numbers of murders. Among the best-known victims was Msgr. Oscar Romero, archbishop of San Salvador, who was killed on March 24, 1980, and immediately venerated as a martyr by Salvadorians, who have given him the title "Saint Romero of America." There were also four US religious murdered in 1980; nine years later, on November 16, 1989, six Jesuits were killed in the Jesuit University in San Salvador, shot down in the little garden of their residence. Today six red rosebushes have been planted in that garden, which has been turned into a memorial of their martyrdom.

Landing in Tegucigalpa, the capital of Honduras, is in itself quite an experience. The city is at the bottom of a steep-sided valley, and the airplane has to skim over the mountain barrier and then plunge down at the last minute onto the runway. Here, too, violence is omnipresent. In a reception district for displaced persons where the Church does a lot of work, the priest who looks after the local church was attacked recently. A laywoman, Dalila, shows me her rosary beads, saying, "This is my weapon!"

Honduran society is extremely unstable, fundamentally because of the breakdown of the family. Many couples are not married, girls become pregnant at sixteen, plenty of people have several partners, as they move from place to place. Nobody looks after the children...

More sects arrive from the United States every day, liking the fact that they have a display-window in a poor country to exhibit when fund-raising back home. These sects spread by offering a salary to committed lay Catholics—catechists, for example—while the Catholic Church does not pay them. Some give in to the temptation.

In Guatemala, after a smoldering civil war lasting thirty-six years (1960–1996), which changed nothing, poverty is on the increase. The effects of climate change and drug-traffickers both arrived a decade ago, and they don't help. The gangrene of drugs brings about generalized corruption, and it is hard to see how the country—or indeed the whole of Central America—can find a cure.

Take the example of a peasant. He has a maize field, which brings him a thousand dollars a year. Drug traders come and tell him: "Now you can make ten thousand dollars; you don't have to worry about anything, and we'll protect you. Either that, or we kill you." The drug traders spread this gangrene over a whole district, supply medicines and food, and provide "protection." Everyone keeps quiet and ends up protecting the drug traders. The forces of law and order also end up being bought.

But the fundamental problem is ultimately the fact that all the country's wealth is in the possession of a tiny minority of people who live in luxury surrounded by a sea of extreme poverty. The nuncio tells me about two or three hundred families who have everything and have no desire for things to change. "Why develop the country? The cake would be bigger, and there would be more people wanting some," he says, expressing their mentality. Of course, there are some rich people who do have a sense of justice, but the system appears to be staying firmly in place.

The inability of the Guatemalans, composed of twenty-four different ethnic groups (which are divided among themselves) to come to any agreement, does not help either. Rigoberta Menchu, Nobel Peace prizewinner for 1992, ran for election, representing the indigenous Guatemalans who make up 62 percent of the population. She only got 3 percent of the vote.

The Church in Guatemala is dynamic, with 60 percent of the country calling themselves Catholic, but she has very limited resources. For example, both of Guatemala City's auxiliary bishops also work as parish priests, simply because there are no funds to pay them otherwise.

Human Ecology Versus the Drug Trade

Today, unanimously and rightly, ecology is recognized as an indispensable concern. It is to be hoped that while thinking of the environment, people also remember the human being. With the aim of achieving real dignity for each person—from conception to natural death—human ecology will be the next major battle for the coming generations.

From this ecological viewpoint, the question may be asked: When will people realize the harm caused by drugs? Physical damage done to drug users aside, how can anyone ignore the tragedies produced by the drug industry?

Beyond the satisfaction of their own need for escape, drug users have to realize that their fix can only reach them over mountains of corpses and rivers of blood. In Mexico alone it is estimated that in the past six years alone, there have been about 50,000 violent deaths linked to drug trafficking, and more than half of that figure occurred in the past two years.

Such being the case, it seems extraordinary for certain government authorities to encourage the use of drugs, even indirectly, by backing and organizing places where users can gather to indulge their habit. Only honest education in the horrifying results of the trade will be able over time to reduce the prevalence of drug use and the tragedies that result from it.

What is more, it seems that the incidence of drug use is leveling off or even declining in rich countries, while it is rising rapidly in poor countries. The problem for the drug traders is that the sale price is lower in poor countries since there is just not as much money available, which means that in the end they risk receiving less income.

It is possible, then, that investment in the drug trade would become less attractive, especially if, at the same time, the law is reinforced in those countries, together with the political will to deal with the scourge of drugs. Obviously that would require a whole set of conditions coming together, but one can always hope.

As for the Church, she is globally respected in those countries and has a stronger voice than in the past now that internal problems linked to conflicting theological options are becoming less acute. There is hope that the Church's work in the field of education, together with her battle for more social justice, will ultimately bear fruit.

V PART

Europe

18

UKRAINE

Lviv, early December 2009. In the middle of a snowstorm, my flight has been delayed, and I am waiting in the gloomy foyer of the city's tiny airport. At last the flight for Kiev is announced. We board the airplane, a Yak 42. It is like being in a 1950s black-and-white film; the cabin is like a museum piece. The runway is covered in snow, and I have to make an act of faith—and hope—in the pilot's skill in flying this antique.

It is my second time in Lviv, this time to write a joint report with KTO (a French-language Catholic television channel). The first time was in September 2005 for the inauguration of the Lviv seminary. A seminary inauguration is something quite rare today, at least in Europe. And that occasion was all the more special because the Greek Catholic Church in the Ukraine, to which the Lviv seminary belongs, had only just escaped total extinction.

Condemned to death by Stalin and violently persecuted until the beginning of the 1990s, there was not much of the Greek Catholic Church left in Ukraine. It was the huge numbers of Ukrainians who had left the country—and undoubtedly the blood of so many martyrs—that enabled this Byzantine-rite Catholic Church to come back to life and grow exponentially in such a short time. Largely financed by ACN, the seminary opened in 2005 and now has more than 200 seminarians, and the standard of teaching and training is extremely high.

A Short-Lived Revolution

The beginning of the twenty-first century saw an unprecedented wave of revolutions, with the countries concerned usually adopting a color or a flower as a symbol of their movement. Examples are roses in Georgia in 2003, tulips in Kyrgyzstan in 2005, and jasmine in Tunisia in 2011; and orange in Ukraine in 2004, blue in Kuwait in 2005, and green in Iran in 2009.

This colorful and even playful aspect might make one forget the seriousness of the changes introduced and what was at stake for the countries' populations, apart from the risks taken by so many people who suddenly came to grips with history. But history is seldom linear, and U-turns are always a possibility. Six years after the orange revolution, Ukraine deleted the colors and decided on a return to Russian uniformity.

In the struggle between the two Viktors for the 2010 presidential election, 5 percent of the vote obtained by Yushchenko, the outgoing president, was the measure of the disappointment that set in after the enthusiasm of the revolution. Viktor Yanukovych, a symbol of the Soviet past and Russian interference in Ukrainian affairs, returned to full power.

The consequences of this turnaround were soon seen: the choice of Mykola Azarov, who spoke Russian and not Ukrainian, as prime minister; the signing of an agreement for the Russian Fleet to retain its base at Sebastopol until 2042; the denial by President Yanukovych of the genocidal nature of the Ukraine famine of 1932–1933 (denial of this genocide is a criminal offense in Ukraine); and the rehabilitation of Stalinism. The direction being taken by Ukraine may be clearly seen.

In the religious sphere, the ecumenical protocol for the president's investiture ceremony was simply ignored, and only Russian Orthodox representatives from Moscow were invited. Patriarch Kyrill came to the investiture, hopefully bringing God's blessing but also unquestionably Moscow's.

In fact Russia had never gotten over the loss of Ukraine. Russia's history is linked to Ukraine's—it was at Kiev that the Rus' was baptized—its agricultural resources rely on supplies from Ukraine, which also provides Russia with access to warmer seas. As for the Orthodox Church, Ukraine represents half of the faithful, as well as half of the resources and half of the patriarchate of Moscow—meaning that here, too, the Russian Church and the Russian State are united as one around a common interest.

As the weeks went by, unease turned into fear. Not only were the Autocephalous Orthodox and Greek Catholics completely ignored, but their churches suffered a wide range of attacks, including burglaries, criminal damage, arson, and homemade bombs.

The early years of Ukraine's independence had witnessed a number of conflicts between religious groups over the ownership of churches, particularly between Orthodox belonging to different jurisdictions, and to a lesser degree between Orthodox and Greek Catholics, but the situation had calmed down. The resurgence of conflicts, and especially the violence that characterized them from 2010 onward, evidenced the new government's aggressiveness in matters of religion.

Then there were cases of intimidation, the most widely known being against Fr. Borys Gudziak, born in the US of Ukrainian parents, a Harvard graduate, and the rector of the Catholic University of Ukraine (which plays an important part in the country, whether it be in the struggle against corruption or in favor of ecumenicalism). Regularly threatened with expulsion, Fr. Gudziak has since been ordained bishop and resides now in Paris, where he takes care of Ukrainian Greek Catholics in France—from Benelux to Switzerland.

There was a new snag in 2014: President Ianoukovitch, who rejected an agreement with the European Union on November 29, 2013, was deposed by the parliament on February 22, 2014, after a demonstration whose bloody repression ended in hundreds of wounded and dozens dead. The new Ukranian government, considered illegitimate by Russia, accused Moscow of "invasion" and of "armed occupation" of Crimea. Whatever it may be, on March 18, 2014, after a referendum held on the 16th, Crimea was annexed by Russia.

Russian neo-imperialism? Defense reaction against the advance of NATO and Western, especially American, provocation? For the general population, the result is the same: The country is once again bruised and torn by a conflict with an uncertain outcome.

Unity at Stake

In the short term there does not seem to be much scope for the "ecumenical action" mentioned above. Indeed, Ukraine is at the very heart of the argument that, according to the Orthodox, divides them from Catholics. It is the country of the former Soviet Union with the largest Byzantine-rite Catholic community, which explains the emphasis placed by the Patriarchate of Moscow on the "Ukrainian problem."

The presence of Greek Catholics seems still more of a threat in that they consider themselves Orthodox, too—the only difference being that they are in communion with the pope in Rome, which makes them Catholics.

But—in the eyes of the Moscow patriarchate—this complicates the Ukrainian ecclesiastical landscape, where there are also two Autocephalous Orthodox churches, one of which derives from Constantinople. Thus there are a total of four Orthodox churches in Ukraine, one of which is in communion with Rome.

Because the Russians would like a monopoly of the religious scene, in Ukraine as in Russia and in all the former satellites of the Russian Empire, this diversity is viewed as a threat—a danger that grows with every ecumenical initiative on the part of the other churches.

For example, the decision of the Greek Catholics and the Ukrainian Autocephalous Orthodox to build a shared church at Kolomyia sounds like a challenge to the Russian Orthodox. For the late Msgr. Simkaylo, Greek Catholic Bishop of Kolomyia, this decision "witnesses to unity between Churches and to Christian love." When the new church was built in a cancer hospital, the bishop saw this as a sign of the unity of believers in the service of those who suffer.

Paradoxically it is quite possible to imagine that here in Ukraine, in spite of everything, Catholics and Orthodox could come closer together, and for that reason, the combat is particularly severe—as it always is when something spiritual is at stake.

The long procession of twentieth-century martyrs, both Catholic and Orthodox, in this country, goes ahead of us in their united witness and prefigures the unity of the Church that Christ asked of us and to which we aspire.

The tensions that we see today, therefore, could be a sign that points to the recovery of unity, announcing not only a great hope but even a return to life.

19

Kosovo

Pristina, capital of Kosovo, mid-September 2012. Autumn is a short time away, but it is still hot and the light is beautiful. The forty-six-mile bus trip from Skopje, the capital of Macedonia, takes two hours. The traffic moves fast, but the border crossing does not. When we arrive in Pristina, it is impossible to miss the bell tower of the huge Cathedral of Mother Teresa, still under construction in the very heart of the city.

Mother Teresa of Pristina

Blessed Mother Teresa of Calcutta, despite her title, was Albanian, like most of the population of Kosovo, although she was born in Skopje. The reason is simply that when she was born in 1910, the borders were different, and the whole region was still part of the Ottoman Empire.

Partly financed by ACN, the imposing building is already making its mark. Unlike a certain type of recent Western theological thought whose watchword seemed to be self-depreciating, the Church in these countries aims to be seen—nothing is too good for God—rather like the medieval-era masterpieces in Europe, which are unrivalled today.

Everything about the cathedral seems huge, so that one wonders if they will ever manage to fill it, but the totality is harmonious. Officially inaugurated in September 2010, in the context of the celebrations for the centennial of Mother Teresa's birth, the cathedral is still very much a work in progress.

The foundation stone was laid by the former President Ibrahim Rugova, and work started in earnest in 2007. Rugova, a Muslim and the emblematic leader of Kosovo's claim to independence, is widely rumored to have been converted to Catholicism before he died.

A Forceps Delivery

After the collapse of Communism, the federation of the former Yugoslavia exploded into seven separate countries—although Kosovo is not yet universally recognized as a country, for obvious diplomatic reasons with regard to the Slavic world, and especially Serbia and Russia. Admittedly Kosovo did not have an entirely "natural birth."

Perhaps the Yugoslav conflict is still too recent, and Western countries' participation in the war, whose causes and ends are still hard to understand, makes the debate more difficult, but I have always found the history of Kosovo doubtful. After my brief stay there in 2012, I still thought it rather ambiguous, but the place made a good impression on me, even though there are still causes for concern.

The first is: What about the sovereignty of nations? With lots of help from the US, a territory about the size of Connecticut was separated from Serbia in order to make a practically single-religion (90 percent Muslim) state in the heart of Europe. What is more, this same process, aptly termed Balkanization, is being repeated in the Middle East today—as though different religions were incapable of living together.

Admittedly there were certain advantages to the United States in this operation, including the weakening of one of Russia's historical allies, the quasi-appropriation of the territory with the setting up of a large US military base (Camp Bondsteel), the exploration of some rich natural underground resources, and the control, as an accessory, of the future AMBO trans-Balkan pipeline, but these considerations where undoubtedly marginal.

Another cause for concern is that there are still around 100,000 Orthodox in Kosovo, about 6 percent of the population, and they no longer have any real problems except in the northwest and especially in Mitrovica, where they are openly persecuted and owe their survival to the strong presence of KFOR (Kosovo Force, a multinational peacekeeping force set up by NATO). Centuries-old churches and historic monasteries have been destroyed, and all this has been done in the middle of Europe.

Finally, corruption, or even mafia-style trafficking, is already spreading like gangrene through a country that does not yet have a properly developed or even functional state structure. Such being the case, one has to wonder about the future of Kosovo without massive and ongoing help from outside. Kosovo's currency, like Montenegro's, is the euro, since the only currency these two new countries had before was the Yugoslav dinar.

We may recall in passing that Yugoslavia was a very prosperous country in the past, easily surpassing its eastern neighbors, Bulgaria, Romania, and Hungary (which were satellites of the Eastern bloc), until well into the 1980s.

◆ ◆ ◆

Despite all this, Kosovo, as I said, made a good impression on me, and the work being done there by the Catholic Church counts for a lot. Although small in numbers—65,000 Catholics, or under 3 percent of the population—the Church is a firm presence in the country and is well regarded. Forty-seven priests look after twenty-five parishes and are helped by about a hundred religious sisters.

Many people, beginning with Muslims, are now finding the Christian faith attractive. According to the local bishop, less than 5 percent of Muslims in Kosovo practice their religion, and the rest do not even know what it consists of. Five centuries of Ottoman occupation ended up by converting the population en masse, but although the majority embraced Islam, Kosovan culture and way of life remain profoundly Christian.

Islam does not have deep roots here. It is true that in these past years, mosques have been built in many villages, all financed from abroad, but as a general rule "only a small number of people gather there for prayer," Fr. Uka tells me.

The same is true of Macedonia and Albania, which, with Kosovo, form the "Albanian connection," three countries with large numbers of Albanians.

In Macedonia, mainly Muslim Albanians account for 28 percent of the population. Christians make up a little over two-thirds of the population—most of them Orthodox, with a very small minority of Catholics. Relations with the Orthodox Church are far from easy.

In Albania, figures have to be treated with caution. An official figure has been given of 70 percent Muslims, but not even the Muslims believe it. In actual fact, the population seems to be about 50 percent Muslim and 50 percent Christians (30 percent Orthodox and 20 percent Catholics).

But after decades of extreme atheism, most Albanians, whether Muslim or Christian, know nothing about their religion. Many "Christians" have never even been baptized. Young people up to about the age of thirty are interested, and so are elderly people, but those aged between forty and sixty do not want to hear about the faith. They have suffered a surfeit of indoctrination and have become impermeable to any ideas, whether political or religious.

Albania, in fact, took the notion of the death of God to the extreme, banning the very word "God." Enver Hoxha, who ruled the country with an iron hand for forty years from 1945 to his death in 1985 and who proclaimed Albania to be the "foremost atheist state in the world" in 1967, did not manage to kill God but took his revenge on the clergy, making a whole cohort of martyrs.

Desperately Seeking Apostles

It would be reasonable to ask how countries that have been so dehumanized, or artificially carved up, will manage to establish any lasting stability, any environment that offers hope for the real development of the human spirit. With recent traumas of different kinds, such a task might well seem beyond them.

There is also the burning question of Albanian identity. "Who are we?" ask Albanians, whether in Albania, Kosovo, or Macedonia. To a greater or lesser degree, they are aware that their roots are Christian, but commitment to the faith, whichever one it is, today needs real conviction.

Whoever can best respond to the spiritual needs of Albanians today will find a broad road opening up. This offers huge potential to the Church, but witnesses are still badly needed. And that is the crux of the matter.

According to the local bishop, in thirty years a large part of the population may have returned to Christianity. He has already personally baptized over three hundred people, and another thirty are preparing for baptism on Easter in the cathedral, but that is only in his parish, and there are plenty of others.

Alban, who studied economics at Pristina University, was baptized recently. "My ancestors were Catholic originally," he said, "so for me, baptism was like a return to the faith of my forebears, a return to my roots."

It is not yet a mass movement, but if the bishop is to be believed, a mass movement will not be long in coming. Will Kosovo be a country with a future for the Church? Meanwhile, Blessed Mother Teresa, the ball is in your court.

20

FRANCE

Champ de Mars, Paris, France, August 19, 1997. World Youth Day in Paris has just begun. Under a blazing sun, the packed crowd that reached from the Eiffel Tower to the military school is cheering John Paul II. This World Youth day marked a real turning point for young French Catholics, who suddenly woke up to the joy of knowing Christ and their holy pride in belonging to the Church. A new generation had arisen: the John Paul II generation.

It was then that the pope announced that he was making a gift to France, as well as to the universal Church: St. Thérèse of Lisieux was to be made a Doctor of the Church during a ceremony on October 19. St. Thérèse wanted to be everything at once: a spouse of Christ in the cloister of her Carmelite convent, a missionary in the Far East, a priest, and a martyr. How could she fail to move young people, who are sometimes disenchanted but always, even subconsciously, in search of the absolute?

On the following Sunday we gathered for the closing Mass of World Youth Day at the Longchamp racecourse. There were more than a million of us there. Who says the Church is about to disappear?

Some years later, I went to weekday Mass in a parish church when the Gospel for the day was the passage where Jesus asks, "When the Son of man comes, will he find faith on earth?" (Luke 18:8). I had heard this Gospel passage before, naturally, but that day it took on a special significance, because I was the only person attending Mass.

The two scenes, in such dramatic contrast, somehow represent our era, when the Church in France sometimes seems to be dwindling to nothing and at the same time shows proofs of astonishing vitality. It is true that numbers have collapsed and practicing Catholics are now a tiny minority. At the same time, who else in France can boast of physically gathering three million people every week?

A Double Anthropological Challenge

Readers may wonder why France figures in this book. I should state from the outset that the Church is not openly persecuted in France, but, as the subtitle is about hope, I thought it relevant to talk about and even conclude with my own country.

Before describing some notes of hope, however, it has to be pointed out that the Church in France is on the receiving end of a kind of aggressiveness that, although it is not actual discrimination, is certainly painful. She is periodically made the target of verbal and written mockery. She has been through it all before, and in the end it helps her to be humble.

But when that mockery becomes constant, vulgar, and frankly offensive, there comes a point where the sacredness of "freedom of speech" is no longer a sufficient excuse. Yes, freedom of speech is a right, but every right brings with it a duty—in this case the duty of respect for other people and their beliefs. Where discrimination comes in is the fact that it is always Catholics who are mocked; the self-styled humorists never dream, or only very exceptionally, of mocking Jews or Muslims.

St. John Paul II and Benedict XVI both invited Catholics, each in their own way, to face up to this minimal form of martyrdom, which could be called, St. Thérèse of Lisieux-style, "the little way of persecution," consisting of being ridiculed and marginalized. This sort of "persecution" does not threaten one's life but only one's comfort, reputation, and respect: We should at least be ready to make that sacrifice.

In France there are sometimes attacks on Jewish or Muslim places of worship or cemeteries, and angry protests by politicians are quite rightly aired on the media. When, however, it is Catholic churches or Christian burial-places that are attacked, nobody is interested; and yet these count for 85 percent of all such attacks. It might be objected that there are obviously far more Christian places of worship and cemeteries in France than Jewish or Muslim ones, yet that does not sufficiently explain the difference in political and media attention.

Additionally, what we see now, both in France and in Europe generally, is a growth in restrictions on freedom of conscience, which is making it more and more difficult to exercise certain professions in accordance with one's faith. In November 2011, in view of the multiplication of specific cases of this kind of discrimination, ACN organized a conference entitled "Will Christianity Still Have a Place in Europe?"

Finally there is a long list of ways in which society is being forcibly changed, which concern everyone since these concern human life and human nature. Bioethical arguments, the defining of the beginning and the end of life, the nature of the embryo, the developing of a contraceptive and abortive mentality (with the claim that contraception reduces abortions, whereas in reality it increases them), gender theory, marriage and adoption for same-sex couples, surrogate mothers, the commercialization of children, who are treated as commodities . . . the list goes on.

These new plans, which bring with them, as their promoters rightly claim, a change in civilization itself, cause the Church to seem overwhelmed by the breadth of attacks on what she understands by human nature—an understanding that was, until very recently, unanimously recognized and shared.

This new civilization, based on a "new human being," is seen by the Church as a terrible regression leading straight to barbarism. She continues to oppose these things separately and together, and her opposition will become more visible and direct as time goes on.

The Church in the United States is confronted with the same radical measures; as American Cardinal George said not long ago: "I expect to die in bed, my successor will die in prison, and his successor will die a martyr in the public square."

Today's environment is overwhelmingly hostile to the Church's positions. This hostility often is the result of ignorance, since most people no longer have the slightest idea or understanding of the anthropological bases for the Church's stance. Sometimes it is the result of real hatred. In this environment, people will reach the point of feeling more sympathy for the second great challenge, Islam, despite the fact that Islam offers a completely different view of man—and woman—and a different model of civilization. Beyond the straightforwardly religious aspect, one is brought face-to-face with a double challenge, one that questions the validity of the whole Christian view of the nature of man.

The same American bishop continued, "*His* successor will pick up the shards of a ruined society and slowly help rebuild civilization, as the Church has done so often in human history."

◆ ◆ ◆

Faced simultaneously with massive apostasy (the abandonment and total oblivion of their ancestors' faith) and demographic collapse (figures for native European populations are nose-diving), Europe is at the same time experiencing an exponential increase in immigration, mainly of Muslims.

The demographic situation in France is not quite as bad as in neighboring countries, but as it hosts the largest Muslim community in Europe, this challenge affects it directly.

A large part of the Muslim community in France, fortunately, is well integrated or in the process of integration, but an active and well-organized minority, encouraged by the apparent political successes of the more radical groups in a certain number of countries, including those of the "Arab Spring," are seeking to take military control of the whole Muslim community, and then go on to a still more daring political strategy. The changing demographics are working in their favor; they only have to bide their time.

Meanwhile, the Church seeks dialogue, which is obviously not just a good thing but indispensable. Only dialogue will enable us to live together. But that dialogue cannot ignore the truth or content itself with pretty phrases. If difficulties—especially the treatment of Christians in majority-Muslim countries—are systematically excluded from discussion, then the only result will be a growing doubt as to the sincerity of the exchange.

In fact, it seems that a false pacifism reigns in this regard, hand-in-hand with a policy of excluding anyone who might dare to question the assumption that everything is for the best in this best of all possible worlds. This attitude may be sincere, but sincerity does not excuse anyone from the need for intelligent thought. The most positive evaluation is that it is an appeasement strategy involving a deliberate decision not to raise subjects that will annoy the other side and so poison the discussion from the outset.

The problem with this is that by not talking about these matters (how Christians are being treated in some Muslim countries) and imposing a denial of reality, the result is the opposite of what is intended. When people see that their rightful concerns are never taken into consideration, they are frustrated and liable to become violent. Those concerns are not imaginary or the result of a persecution complex—the situation in majority-Muslim countries is really disturbing, and it is difficult not to draw a parallel with the growth of Islam here in the West.

What really needs to be done is to put these concerns on the table, calmly and clearly, so that everyone is able to see the facts objectively. This educational task could—and even should—be offered by the Church, who would gain legitimacy and credibility and earn gratitude for witnessing to the truth and working constructively for peace.

After all justice and peace go hand-in-hand, and it is hard to see how peace can be brought about while situations of injustice are being covered up. It simply does not make sense to call for dialogue and at the same time block any reference to the persecution being endured by Christians in the Middle East.

Specifically the Church in France was noticeably silent about the persecution of Christians behind the Iron Curtain, only a couple hundred miles away. And since that time she has not expressed any repentance for this silence. While it lasted, it was better not to talk about it. And it was better not to talk about it afterward either, with the excuse that it was all in the past and we must turn over a new page and move on. Have courage; will run. Christians are being persecuted? That's just too bad. Are we going to repeat all of that for the Christians in the Middle East, Nigeria, and elsewhere?

We Need Priests!

France has one of the lowest percentages of practicing Catholics anywhere in the world, but the "faithful remnant" is not yet buried. In reality the Church in France has a number of real assets that make her much stronger than she might seem at first sight. In Europe, it could even be claimed that it is the Church in France that offers most reasons for hope.

This is not surprising, considering the fact that she is "the eldest daughter of the Church." God is faithful, and his blessings are irrevocable. In view of this special blessing, there is nothing surprising in the fact that the Church in France has been subjected to severe trials; that too is to be expected. Personally I am convinced that she will once again shine.

There are many signs of resurrection: the demographic vitality and spiritual depths of families of practicing Catholics, the growth of movements deriving from the Charismatic Renewal, the dynamism of communities attached to the

Extraordinary Form of the Roman Rite, and the multiplication of pastoral initiatives at the parish level.

And there are also, quite simply, Catholics themselves. Confronted with a more aggressive environment, the Church is closing ranks and mobilizing. By way of example, the political initiatives that aim at destroying the nature of marriage have aroused, as never before, an awareness of belonging to a living body that has something to say and has the strength to say it. In this sense one could almost feel grateful to Mme. Taubira for having succeeded in awakening the Church in France! (As Minister of Justice, Mme. Christiane Taubira introduced the bill that became Law 2013-404, which legalized same-sex marriage in France.)

I know a young Iranian woman who converted to Christianity and had to flee her country because of death threats. She once told me that she loved Ayatollah Khomeini. When I showed surprise, she explained that, thanks to him, nobody in Iran can stand the ayatollahs. Well, Catholics in France can say something similar. Taubira is our Khomeini.

◆ ◆ ◆

To illustrate the vitality of the Church in France, there is also the development of the catechumenate and the three thousand or so adult baptisms every year, which include more and more former Muslims. This also is happening in the Middle East and in the rest of the world, but particularly in France.

The phenomenon is all the more surprising in that it is dangerous. Apostasy from Islam is forbidden and can be punished with death. Pressure and threats are applied to everyone contemplating such a step, and this is the reason for the extreme caution, even secrecy, especially towards members of one's own family. In these circumstances there are many who stop at an inner conversion and never take the public step of baptism.

It is, however, possible to imagine that, as their numbers increase, the day will come when they will step out of the shadows to claim freedom of choice. Some ex-Muslim converts to Catholicism already estimate that they are one of the most active groups in defending the Church in France, and they believe they also will be at the head of the mission to their former co-religionists.

This is undoubtedly a field of apostolate in which the Church in France should invest resources right now, at least in terms of structures of welcome, since such people often need specialized accompanying. This should be done without "proselytizing," but also without refusing to help, using the excuse of a false dialogue ("Why convert? Islam is fine . . ."). The very least that can be done is to enable those who have already begun the journey to find answers to the questions they ask. At present, a number of them end up joining Evangelical churches, where they feel welcomed and at least people look after them.

◆ ◆ ◆

While it is true that more and more churches are being closed, sold, or demolished, there are also churches being built. For instance, in 2013 work started on a church at Arnouville, near Paris. It is to be a parish church for the Chaldeans, an Eastern Catholic rite from the Middle East and especially Iraq. The Chaldeans around Arnouville already have two big churches, but these are not enough. It is a dynamic and growing community, which is something for everyone to rejoice at.

The liturgy is in Aramaic, and some of the parishioners are Turkish, but in general the people switch happily between French and Arabic. If you add to that all the Lebanese (in 2012 a Maronite diocese was created in France) and make the connection with all the converts whose origins lie in North Africa, this amounts to a growing number of Arab-speaking Catholics in France. The day may come when there are Masses being said in Arabic in France, and this would be just one more reversal of history, of which God is ultimately Lord.

◆ ◆ ◆

In actual fact, however, it is French that will enable all these different communities to come together, including the "faithful remnant" described above and the many other French people who may well discover or rediscover a taste for prayer and for the Catholic faith.

After rejecting everything it could happen that tomorrow people will reject their own generalized rejection and, in the rubble of the nihilistic chaos around them, will come to marvel at the incredible breath of fresh air that is faith in Christ.

Christianity is essentially revolutionary, because the gospel is subversive to the spirit of the world, even though people have forgotten this. Christianity has a deeply liberating purpose and offers unique answers that make sense to the concerns of people today.

The numbers of practicing Catholics may grow faster than we can envisage at present. Where will our churches be then? And where will we find priests? They are in short supply today, so one can only wonder what it will be like ten or twenty years hence. We need priests!

Apart from people who are ideologically committed to violent anti-Christian hatred, one can conceive, and even observe already, a certain curiosity about Christianity and a positive rediscovery of its foundations and the culture it transmits.

◆ ◆ ◆

But beyond culture what matters is a personal encounter, and therefore a real conversion, which can only come about and be spread through contact with Christians who bear witness right where they are, and this is where the witnesses of our time come in: the martyrs of the faith throughout the world today.

Their witness, as we see every day in ACN, touches people and leads them to start asking questions. Their faithfulness to Christ amidst hardship and the very worst trials does not fail to bear fruit—the fruit of conversion and love for Christ. And we realize once again they have much more to give us than we can give them.

In spite of all difficulties, and when it would be in their interest to abandon Jesus Christ, these witnesses reveal to us the treasure they will not renounce: the Person in whom they have put their trust—a trust that does not deceive and gives birth to hope.

Epilogue

Luang Prabang, formerly the imperial capital of Laos. Overhanging the Mekong River, it is a magnificent site and attracts plenty of tourists. What it lacks, however, is a church. Before the "liberation" of the country in 1975 by "people's democratic" forces, there were three churches, but they have all been commandeered.

The priest in charge of this region was appointed apostolic administrator in 1999 and ranks with the bishops. In 2010, the Vatican actually wanted to make him a vicar apostolic, meaning he would have been ordained a bishop, but the priest preferred, and still prefers, to wait. He believes the time is not yet right, and he does not wish to worsen the already tense situation.

His "bishop's palace" consists of a simple house he hopes to turn into a lodging house so he can receive more people. Mass is celebrated quietly in the living room. About fifty faithful come to Mass regularly. The local authorities are not happy, but the priest says he just cannot turn them away.

In his entire vicariate, there are still seven churches left. He only has one other priest to help him, but there are eight seminarians preparing to take up the work, and these are his consolation. In the villages, the faithful may have Mass four times a year. The "bishop" looks prematurely old. He has already had three experiences of being in Laotian prisons, and he lost an eye while breaking stones during his detainment for "reeducation."

The only visible presence of the Church in Luang Prabang consists of three Laotian religious sisters belonging to an order founded in France, the Sisters of Charity of Besançon. Their charism is education. They have a school for deaf-mutes, supported by the government, which makes no provision of its own for people with disabilities. This enables the sisters to be there and even wear their religious habits.

Here, as elsewhere, the Church, reduced to the barest minimum in terms of self-expression, aims to serve the poorest of the poor. Obviously these fifty or so deaf-mutes make no difference to the economy of Laos. But Christians can see in this project the application of charity which, however small it seems, proceeds from the very love of Christ, and that makes it hugely fruitful, far beyond its appearances. But without the religious aspect, it is a fact that this work of service quite simply makes the world more human. When the poorest and weakest are taken into consideration, everyone else discovers that they, too, have their place.

These brave sisters with their semi-clandestine "bishop" are really the treasure of the Church. "Our persecuted brethren are the Church's elite," said Fr. Werenfried, founder of ACN. Being somehow on the front line of the battle waged unceasingly between the forces of evil and the Church, persecuted Christians carry the cross in a very special way.

These are the Christians in danger, very close to the cross—and therefore very close to Christ. That place is one that nobody can take away from them.